Heidegger: A Very Short Introduction

VERY SHORT INTRODUCTIONS are for anyone wanting a stimulating and accessible way into a new subject. They are written by experts, and have been translated into more than 45 different languages.

The series began in 1995, and now covers a wide variety of topics in every discipline. The VSI library currently contains over 550 volumes—a Very Short Introduction to everything from Psychology and Philosophy of Science to American History and Relativity—and continues to grow in every subject area.

Very Short Introductions available now:

Available soon:

For more information visit our website

www.oup.com/vsi/

Michael Inwood

HEIDEGGER

A Very Short Introduction

SECOND EDITION

OXFORD
UNIVERSITY PRESS

OXFORD
UNIVERSITY PRESS

Great Clarendon Street, Oxford, OX2 6DP,
United Kingdom

Oxford University Press is a department of the University of Oxford.
It furthers the University's objective of excellence in research, scholarship,
and education by publishing worldwide. Oxford is a registered trade mark of
Oxford University Press in the UK and in certain other countries

First published 1997 as an Oxford University Press paperback
First published as a Very Short Introduction 2000
Second edition published 2019

Impression: 4

Published in the United States of America by Oxford University Press
198 Madison Avenue, New York, NY 10016, United States of America

British Library Cataloguing in Publication Data

Data available

Library of Congress Control Number: 2018958811

ISBN 978-0-19-882866-2

Printed in Great Britain by
Ashford Colour Press Ltd., Gosport, Hampshire.

Contents

Heidegger

List of illustrations

Abbreviations and referencing

All references to *Being and Time* (BT) are to the pages of the German editions of *Sein und Zeit*. This pagination is indicated in the margins of the English translations, *Being and Time*, tr. J. Macquarrie and E. Robinson (Oxford, 1962), whose translations I adopt with some amendments, and tr. J. Stambaugh (New York, 1996, 2010). Volumes of the complete edition of Heidegger's works, the *Gesamtausgabe*, published by Vittorio Klostermann of Frankfurt am Main from 1975 on, are referred to by the volume number in lower-case roman numerals, followed by the page reference. (The German pagination is again indicated in the translations.) The volumes referred to, with the dates of *(a)* the original delivery of the lectures, *(b)* the publication of the *Gesamtausgabe* edition, are:

xvii	*Einführung in die phänomenologische Forschung* (*Introduction to Phenomenological Research*, tr. D. Dahlstrom (Bloomington, Ind., 2005)) *(a)* 1923–4; *(b)* 1994
xx	*Prolegomena zur Geschichte des Zeitbegriffs* (*History of the Concept of Time: Prolegomena*, tr. T. Kisiel (Bloomington, Ind., 1985)) *(a)* 1925; *(b)* 1979
xxi	*Logik: Die Frage nach der Wahrheit* (*Logic: The Question of Truth*, tr. T. Sheehan (Bloomington, Ind., 2010)) *(a)* 1925–6; *(b)* 1976
xxii	*Grundbegriffe der Antiken Philosophie* (*Basic Concepts of Ancient Philosophy*, tr. R. Rojcewicz (Bloomington, Ind., 2010)) *(a)* 1926; *(b)* 1993

Heidegger

lxv   *Beiträge zur Philosophie (Vom Ereignis)*
        (Contributions to Philosophy (From Enowning), tr.
        P. Emad and K. Maly (Bloomington, Ind., 1999))
        (a) written 1936–8; *(b)* 1989

Other works, all by Heidegger unless otherwise specified, are referred
to by the following abbreviations:

Arendt	H. Arendt, 'Martin Heidegger at Eighty', *New York Review of Books* (21 October 1971)
BN	'Black Notebooks', *Ponderings* II–VI, VII–XI, XII–XV, tr. R. Rojcevicz (Bloomington, IND, 2016–17) (written 1931–8, 1938–9, 1939–41)
CM	E. Husserl, *Cartesian Meditations: An Introduction to Phenomenology*, tr. D. Cairns (The Hague, 1973) (written in 1929)
CT	*The Concept of Time*, tr. W. McNeill (Oxford, 1992) (lecture given in 1924)
ER	*The Essence of Reasons*, tr. T. Malick (Evanston, 1969) (first published 1929)
HEP	'Hölderlin and the Essence of Poetry', tr. D. Scott, in *Existence and Being*, ed. W. Brock (Chicago, 1949) (lecture given in Rome in 1936)
IM	*An Introduction to Metaphysics*, tr. R. Manheim (New Haven, 1959) (first published 1953, but based on lectures from 1935)
IN	R. G. Collingwood, *The Idea of Nature* (Oxford, 1945)
LH	'Letter on Humanism', tr. F. Capuzzi, in M. Heidegger, *Basic Writings*, ed. D. Krell (New York, 1977, 1993), 141–81 (written 1946, first published 1947)
Löwith	K. Löwith, *My Life in Germany Before and After 1933: A Report*, tr. E. King (London, 1994)
MWP	'My Way to Phenomenology', in *On Time and Being*, tr. J. Stambaugh (New York, 1972), 74–82 (first published 1963)

NI–II and Ni–iv	*Nietzsche*, in two volumes, tr. D. E. Krell in four volumes (New York, 1979) (first published 1961, but based on lectures of 1936–40)
NHS	*Nature, History, State: 1933–1934*, tr. G. Fried and R. Polt (London, 2015)
OWA	'The Origin of the Work of Art', in Martin Heidegger, *Poetry, Language, Thought*, tr. A. Hofstadter (New York, 1975), 17–87 (first published 1950 in Heidegger's *Holzwege* (*Woodpaths*))
OWL	*On the Way to Language*, tr. P. D. Hertz and J. Stambaugh (New York, 1971) (first published 1959)
PR	*The Principle of Reason*, tr. R. Lilly (Bloomington, Ind., 1991) (lectures given in 1956, first published 1957)
T	'The Thing', in M. Heidegger, *Poetry, Language, Thought*, tr. A. Hofstadter (New York, 1975), 161–84 (lecture of 1950, first published 1951)

I have sometimes altered the translations given in the above works.

Chapter 1
Heidegger's life

He was (with the possible exception of Wittgenstein) the greatest philosopher of the 20th century. He was (with the possible exception of Hegel) the greatest charlatan ever to claim the title of 'philosopher', a master of hollow verbiage masquerading as profundity. He was an irredeemable German redneck, and, for a time, a gullible and self-important Nazi. He was a pungent, if inevitably covert, critic of Nazism, a discerning analyst of the ills

1. Messkirch, 1820.

2. Heidegger as a schoolboy, in about 1899.

of our age and our best hope of a cure for them. Each of these claims has been advanced, with greater or lesser plausibility, on Heidegger's behalf. Who was the man who provokes these contrasting reactions?

Martin Heidegger was born on 26 September 1889 to a poor Catholic family in Messkirch in Baden in south-west Germany (see Figure 1). His father was cellarman and sexton of the local church. In 1903 Martin went to the high school at Konstanz, where he was supported by a scholarship and lived in a Catholic boarding-house (see Figure 2). He was now being prepared for the priesthood. In 1906 he moved to the high school in Freiburg where the Church gave him free board and lodging. Here his interest in philosophy was first aroused, by a work called *On the Various Meanings of Being According to Aristotle* (1862), by Franz Brentano, one of the forebears of the phenomenological movement. Later he came across Carl Braig's *On Being: An Outline of Ontology* (1896), containing excerpts from Aristotle and medieval philosophers such as Aquinas (MWP, 74). In 1909 he left high school and became a Jesuit novice, but was discharged within a month owing to heart trouble and perhaps his lack of spiritual vocation. He then entered Freiburg University, and studied theology and scholastic philosophy.

2

In 1911 he underwent a crisis that led him to break off his training for the priesthood and turn to philosophy and the moral and natural sciences. He now studied modern philosophy, especially the *Logical Investigations* of Edmund Husserl, the leading figure in the phenomenological movement, whose aim was systematic enquiry into our conscious mental processes without regard to their non-mental causes and consequences. He graduated in 1913 with a dissertation on *The Theory of the Judgement in Psychologism*, in which he criticized, in the spirit of Husserl, attempts to analyse the logical notion of a judgement in terms of psychology. In 1915 his habilitation thesis on *Duns Scotus's Theory of Categories and Meaning* qualified him to lecture at the university.

Heidegger's academic career was interrupted by World War I. In 1915 he was conscripted, but regarded as unsuitable for combat duties and assigned to the postal and meteorological services. In 1917 he married a Protestant, Elfriede Petri, and, shortly after the birth of their son Jorg in January 1919, he announced his breach with the 'system of Catholicism'. (See Figure 3) On his discharge from the army in 1918 he had become an unsalaried lecturer at Freiburg and an assistant to Husserl, who had become professor at the university in 1916. Heidegger now began to win fame as a teacher of brilliance and insight. His lectures on Aristotle, St Paul,

3. **Heidegger with Elfriede and their sons in 1924.**

St Augustine, phenomenology, the world of our everyday experience, and the human being, won him acclaim as the 'hidden king' of philosophy (Arendt).

In 1923 he moved to Marburg as associate professor and there befriended the theologian Rudolf Bultmann and began an enduring relationship with Hannah Arendt (see Figure 4).

4. Hannah Arendt, in about 1930.

(His friendship and correspondence with Karl Jaspers had begun in 1920.) At Marburg he extended the range of his lectures with courses on Aristotle's *Rhetoric*, Plato's *Sophist*, Presocratic Greek philosophy, time, truth, Aquinas, Kant, and Leibniz. He had not, however, published for ten years. Then in the spring of 1927 he published his great work, *Being and Time* (BT), in the *Yearbook for Philosophy and Phenomenological Research*, edited by Husserl, and also as a separate volume. His reason for publishing it was, he said, to meet government requirements for appointment to a full professorship at Marburg (MWP, 80).

In the following year he succeeded Husserl to the chair at Freiburg. His inaugural lecture, in 1929, was entitled 'What is Metaphysics?'—a subject on which he lectured at greater length in the following winter (though, in his characteristic manner, much of his course on 'The Fundamental Concepts of Metaphysics' is devoted to the apparently extraneous topics of boredom and insects). In that year too he engaged in public debate with Ernst Cassirer on Kant's philosophy and published *Kant and the Problem of Metaphysics*. He also lectured on the German idealists Schelling and Hegel, the allegory of the cave in Plato's *Republic*, and the Presocratic philosophers Anaximander and Parmenides. In 1930 he rejected an offer of a chair in Berlin. Heidegger was deeply attached to the provincial life of southern Germany, to its small towns and rugged landscape—he did much of his writing in a mountain cottage at Todtnauberg, which he built in 1923 (see Figures 5 and 6). He disliked big cities and their social and cultural life.

The Weimar Republic, from 1918 to 1933, was marked by intense cultural activity, but also by economic distress and political turmoil. In September 1930 Adolf Hitler's National Socialist German Workers' Party (NSDAP, but commonly known as 'Nazi') became the second largest party in Germany. On 30 January 1933 Hitler was appointed chancellor in a right-wing coalition. The Reichstag fire on 27 February gave him an excuse for rushing

5. Heidegger with Elfriede in their cottage.

through decrees conferring absolute power on the Nazi party. On 30 June 1934, on the pretext of Ernst Röhm's rebellion, he murdered his rivals, Röhm's Storm Troopers, and other inconvenient party members, such as Gregor Strasser, a 'left-wing' Nazi more opposed to capitalism than to Jews or Bolshevism. (Josef Goebbels had been a supporter of Strasser, but was converted by Hitler in 1926 to a programme that could win the backing of bankers and industrialists.) On 2 August 1934 Hitler was proclaimed 'Führer of the German Reich' ('Leader of the German Empire').

In the 1920s Heidegger was virtually apolitical, but by the early 1930s he had become sympathetic to Nazism. On 21 April 1933 he was elected rector of Freiburg University by the faculty, and on 1 May joined the NSDAP. On 27 May he delivered his rectoral address, 'The Self-Affirmation of the German University', which, though not an especially reassuring document, is noticeably free of antisemitism. (He did, however, place labour, military service, and knowledge on an equal footing as duties of students.)

6. Heidegger outside the cottage.

As rector Heidegger cooperated with the new regime, while trying
to moderate some of its cruder aspects. He campaigned for
Germany's withdrawal from the League of Nations in the plebiscite
of November 1933. Conflicts with the faculty and party officials led
him to resign as rector in April 1934 and, though perforce he
remained in the party, he took no further significant part in

politics. He later claimed that he became disillusioned with Nazism after the Röhm *putsch*.

Heidegger published little in the 1930s but continued to lecture. In 1935 he spoke, in Freiburg, on 'The Origin of the Work of Art'. He went to Rome in 1936 to give the first of many lectures on Hölderlin, the cryptic philosophical poet who was Hegel's room-mate at the Tübingen theological college in the late 18th century. In Rome he met Karl Löwith, a former pupil of Jewish descent, who claimed that Heidegger retained his allegiance to Nazism (Löwith, 59–61). In the same year he began lectures on Nietzsche, which continued into the early 1940s and were published in 1961. Heidegger's friends claim that these lectures covertly criticized Nazism and tried to rescue Nietzsche from the use made of him to support racism. Heidegger was now under surveillance by the Gestapo.

From 1938 technology assumed a larger role in his thought. This interest appeared in a Freiburg lecture of 1938, 'The Establishment of the Modern World-Picture by Metaphysics' and also in a seminar on Ernst Jünger's essay 'The Worker'. (Jünger was neither a Nazi nor anti-Semitic, but some of his ideas, such as 'total mobilization', were adopted by the Nazis.) Heidegger's lectures in this period often refer to political events and later to the war. He always relates them to the 'forgetfulness of Being' and to technology. The wilful construction of a world-empire to last for millennia shows, he argued, a preference for quantity over quality that is alien to genuine creators like the Greeks. Empire-building stems not primarily from 'dictators' and 'authoritarian states', but from the 'metaphysical essence of modernity', the will to mastery over nature (li. 17f.). This verdict was delivered in the summer of 1941, at the height of Hitler's power.

In the autumn of 1944 Heidegger was (humiliatingly) drafted into the *Volkssturm* (the 'People's Storm', something like the British

Home Guard or 'Dad's Army') to help dig anti-tank ditches along the Rhine. At the beginning of 1945 he went to Messkirch to arrange and secure his manuscripts. In June, two months after Germany's collapse, he appeared before the 'Denazification Commission' in Freiburg. Officers of the French occupying forces contacted him and made arrangements for him to meet his long-time admirer Jean-Paul Sartre. This plan miscarried, but he corresponded with Sartre and struck up a friendship with Jean Beaufret, the most loyal of French Heideggerians. In 1946 he was forbidden to teach; the ban lasted until 1949. He was permitted to keep his library and was granted an emeritus professorship. This verdict, based partly on a report by Jaspers (an old friend opposed to Nazism), was supported by the university and the French administration.

Heidegger's career as a writer and lecturer soon revived. He presented 'What are Poets for?' (1946) to a small audience in memory of Rilke's death twenty years earlier. He published *On Humanism* (1947), a letter to Beaufret in which he distanced himself from French existentialism. In December 1949 he gave four lectures to the Bremen Club, one of which, 'The Thing', was delivered at the Bavarian Academy of Fine Arts in 1950. He renewed old friendships: Arendt visited him in 1950, and his correspondence with her, and also with Jaspers, revived. He lectured again to the Bavarian Academy in 1953, on 'The Question of Technology'. He travelled more widely than hitherto. He lectured on 'What is Philosophy?' at Cérisy-la-Salle in 1955, and later on 'Hegel and the Greeks' (1957) at Aix-en-Provence. He befriended artists such as Georges Braque (see Figure 7), and poets such as Rene Char, a former French resistance fighter. On his seventieth birthday in 1959 he became an honorary citizen of Messkirch. He visited Greece for the first time in 1962, and again in 1967, when he addressed the Academy of Sciences and Arts in Athens on 'The Source of Art and the Vocation of Thinking'. From 1966 to 1973 he gave several seminars, in

7. Heidegger with Georges Braque, Varengeville, 1955.

Le Thor in Provence and later in Zaehringen. He attempted to justify his conduct during the Nazi era in an interview with *Der Spiegel* in 1966. This was published after his death ten years later, and bears the title 'Only a god can save us', a remark he made in the interview which recalls a poem of Hölderlin: 'In my boyhood days | Often a god would save me | From the shouts and the rod of men'.

After the war, Heidegger had steadily published works that were mainly revised versions of lectures. In his last days he helped to prepare a complete edition of his works, which was to include his lectures as well as works published earlier. He declared his wish that no thought he had expressed in a lecture would be lost. A volume of this edition appeared in 1975, containing Marburg lectures on 'The Basic Problems of Phenomenology' from the summer of 1927. (The edition is now virtually complete; it fills over a hundred volumes.) Heidegger died in 1976 on 26 May, and was buried on 28 May in the churchyard at Messkirch beside his parents (see Figure 8). A Catholic mass was held in his memory. The officiating priest, his nephew Heinrich Heidegger, quoted Jeremiah 1:7: 'But the Lord said unto me, Say not, I am a child: for thou shalt go to all that I shall send thee, and whatsoever I command thee thou shalt speak.'

8. Heidegger's grave in the Messkirch cemetery.

Heidegger's life is an intriguing tale of a wanderer's return, but what makes it more interesting than many other such lives is his status as a thinker. No one would fret over the details of his political activity, let alone his religious beliefs or private life, were he not a significant philosopher. To his philosophy, then, we now turn.

Chapter 2
Heidegger's philosophy

Heidegger's admirers differ over whether he produced a *second* great work, and if so, which it is; the Nietzsche lectures or the *Contributions to Philosophy (Of the Event)*, drafted between 1936 and 1938, but published only in 1989, as well as other works, are often nominated. But there is general agreement that he wrote one great work, and that it is BT.

BT bears comparison with Hegel's *Phenomenology of Spirit*, if not with Plato's *Republic* or Kant's *Critique of Pure Reason*. It is by far the most influential of his writings: it has left its mark on theologians, psychologists, and sociologists as well as philosophers. It crystallizes the results of his reading, lecturing, and thinking over the previous decade, and points the way ahead to his later works, which, whatever their divergences from BT, cannot be understood without it. It is, however, one of the most difficult books ever written. Its overall structure and its language present problems to the reader, especially the non-German reader.

The argument of the work is this: it is important to ask the question 'What is Being?', a question which was once asked but has long been forgotten. To do this we need to consider some being or entity, and the obvious choice is the human being or 'Dasein', since that is the being that asks the question and has a preconceptual understanding of Being which, if used with caution, will guide us towards an answer to our question. So the first section of the book undertakes a 'preparatory fundamental analysis of Dasein', which argues that Dasein is essentially 'in the world' and that its Being is 'care'. In the second section he introduces a theme which was only implicit in the first: time. Dasein is essentially temporal: it looks ahead to its own death, it surveys its life as a whole in conscience and resoluteness, it is essentially historical. Dasein's Being is intimately linked with temporality.

BT was originally intended to have a third section considering the question of Being as such and its relationship to time, in greater independence of Dasein. This section never appeared, but the preface to the seventh edition of BT (1953) refers us to his *Introduction to Metaphysics* (1953), which raises the question why there are beings rather than nothing, and considers the connections between Being, on the one hand, and, on the other, becoming, appearance, thinking, and ought. (In a marginal note to his copy of BT, he refers to *The Basic Problems of Phenomenology* (1927, 1975), as a substitute for the missing third section. This work is itself incomplete, dealing with little over a half of its promised contents.)

BT was also intended to have a second part, itself in three sections, dealing respectively with Kant, Descartes, and Aristotle. (Heidegger likes to do the history of philosophy backwards: a philosopher is unmasked to reveal the face of a predecessor on whom he covertly depends, a face which is in turn exposed as a mask, and so on.) This part too did not appear, but other works and lectures give a better picture of its intended contents than we have of the missing section of the first part.

Even this brief survey of BT raises questions about it. What is the question of Being and why is it important to ask it? What is Dasein and how is it related to the question of Being? How is

Dasein in the world? Why are time and temporality crucial to Dasein and its Being? What did Heidegger propose to say in the missing parts of BT and how, if at all, is it related to his later works? These and other questions will be considered in the following chapters.

Chapter 3
Being

The term 'Being' enters into a variety of contrasts. It contrasts, firstly, with 'knowledge' and with 'science'. Many philosophers in Heidegger's day and earlier, especially those claiming to follow Kant, were concerned mainly with epistemology or the theory of knowledge, asking such questions as 'What can we know?' and 'What are the foundations of the sciences?' Heidegger was averse to epistemology: it 'continually sharpens the knife but never gets round to cutting' (lviii. 4). Knowledge, especially scientific knowledge, involves a relation—knowing—between a knower and an object, or range of objects, known. Heidegger's doubts concern each of these three elements.

Take first the knower. What is it? Is it a pure subject wholly absorbed in the disinterested, theoretical knowledge of its subject matter, or is it an interested human being, situated in a particular place and a particular time, with many other relations and attitudes to many other things than the objects of its science? Take secondly the relation of knowing. Why knowing? Knowing is only one relation among many that we adopt to worldly things; it is not the first relation we adopt, it is taken up fairly late in one's career, and then only sporadically; nor is it the most obvious attitude to take towards one's spouse or the key to one's front door.

How is knowing related to these other attitudes? What does knowing consist in? We tend to speak as if knowing were uniform, as if electrons were known in the same way as historical events. Or if we notice that this is not so we are tempted, like Descartes, to propose an ideal form of knowledge that will guarantee unerring results about, say, the dimensions and movements of material particles. But this will not do for, say, historical events, which are thereby excluded from the realm of knowable objects. If we decline this course, then we realize that the right way of getting to know about a range of entities depends in part on the nature or Being of those entities. We know about historical events in one way, and about electrons in another: we do not sift documents to find out about electrons or try to detect Napoleon in a laboratory. This is because historical events are a different sort of entity from electrons. So before we deal with knowledge, we need to consider the nature, or the Being, of the object known.

Objects or entities fall into classes: numbers, plants, stars, animals, and so on. A class of entities is often the preserve of a special science. The astronomer studies stars, the botanist plants, and so on. If the philosopher is to study Being rather than knowledge, should he also study stars and plants, differing from the scientific specialist only in the breadth and generality of his knowledge, with its attendant superficiality? No. This would not only consign the philosopher to a lower status than Heidegger is ready to tolerate, it would miss a prior, more fundamental question about the objects of the sciences. How do we come to divide up the world of entities in this way? The world does not naturally present itself to us carved up in readiness for the sciences. When two lovers walk hand in hand across a meadow under a starry sky, they do not see themselves and their surroundings as objects separated out for the geologist, the botanist, the meteorologist, even if they are themselves, say, geologists in their professional lives. Once there were no such refined boundaries between the objects of different sciences as

16

there now are. Even in recent times scientists sometimes redefine the nature of their subject matter: they redraw the boundary around it, form a new conception of what lies within it, open up new ways of knowing about their objects, and close off old ones. Such a scientist is projecting a view of Being onto entities, a projection of a sort that underlies any science.

This raises another problem. If the scientist, at least the reflective, innovative scientist, considers the Being of his subject matter, what is there left for the philosopher to do? Why not leave it to the scientist? Because, Heidegger argues, the scientist is concerned only with one among several 'regions' of beings; as a scientist he ignores the background against which projection takes place, the objects left for other sciences and the familiar articles of use we rely on every day, but which elude the theoretical sciences altogether. Not to mention the nature of Being as such or the informal overall understanding of Being that enables us to highlight one area of Being in particular.

The various meanings of Being

Heidegger may have convinced us that we should focus on entities rather than on our knowledge or on the sciences. But 'Being' contrasts not only with knowledge, but also with 'beings' or 'entities'. Why *Being* rather than beings? We know of old that the verb 'to be' has different uses or senses: the existential, the predicative, and the 'is' of identity. Why should we regard this as of central importance to the sciences or as the main, perhaps the only, genuine philosophical question? The scientist can decide *that* certain entities *are* (the existential 'is') and *what* they are (the predicative 'is'). What more do scientists or philosophers have to do with Being? But Being is not, Heidegger argues, the thin, unappetizing subject that it has come to seem. To see this we need to look at the 'various meanings of Being' that he found in Brentano's book on Aristotle and later in Aristotle himself.

17

According to Aristotle the verb 'to be' is ambiguous in several dimensions. When we say that something is (such-and-such or a so-and-so), we may mean that it is actually or that it is potentially. (For Aristotle actuality is logically prior to potentiality.) Again, 'to be' sometimes amounts to 'to be true, to be the case'. Most importantly the meaning of 'to be' varies with the category of the entity to which it is applied. Aristotle proposed ten categories, of which the most fundamental is substance, while items in the others—quality, quantity, relation, and so on—depend for their Being on substances. Everything there is falls into one or other of these categories, so that they are classes or genera of entities. But they are, on Aristotle's view, the highest genera that there are. Beings as a whole do not constitute a genus, since 'Being' is ambiguous: we can see this, if we consider that a substance, such as a horse, simply *is*, while a quality, such as its brown colour, is the colour *of* the horse, its Being depends on that of the substance to which it belongs.

An equivocal term cannot demarcate a genus, however. Aristotle's example of this is the word 'healthy'. 'Healthy' means 'possessing health' (healthy people), 'conducive to health' (healthy food), and 'manifesting health' (healthy appetite). Things that are healthy in all these senses cannot constitute a single genus, because something that is healthy in one sense may be unhealthy in another: healthy food, such as a roast chicken, produces health in us, but it no longer possesses health itself, or a healthy appetite, though it manifests health, may not be conducive to health. The word 'healthy' is not utterly ambiguous; its senses are systematically and significantly related to each other, having, Aristotle suggests, a unity of 'analogy'. And this may be true of the word 'being'. Like 'healthy', 'being' does not demarcate a single genus, but it is sufficiently unified to constitute a single topic of enquiry, in a way that, say, the different types of 'bank' (river banks and money banks) do not.

Being acquired further refinements in its later history—the medieval distinction, for example, between Being as essence and Being as existence, which does not emerge clearly in Aristotle.

But enough has been said to set the stage for Heidegger. He agreed with Aristotle that there were different types of Being, if not exactly different senses of 'being'. He introduces for this a third term alongside 'that'-being, the fact *that* something is or exists, and 'what'-being, what that thing is: 'how'-being, the mode, manner, or type of an entity's Being.

If we remain within the confines of Aristotle's categories, we have, firstly, the fact that horses exist, secondly those features of horse distinguishing it from other animals and from other substances in general, and finally its mode of Being, the fact that it is a substance, not an entity in some other category. Or, to take a case beyond the confines of Aristotle's categories, while mathematicians study the 'that' and 'what' of numbers, asking whether, say, there is a greatest prime number, or whether every even number is the sum of two primes, philosophers ask about the Being of numbers, about *how* they are or their way of Being (cf. xxii. 8, 43; xx. 149). We may answer, as Husserl did, that numbers are neither physical nor psychological entities, but 'ideal' rather than 'real' entities. In that case, their mode of Being is ideality rather than reality.

Heidegger versus Aristotle

If Aristotle and his successors have done so much work on the question of Being, what more can Heidegger do? Often he suggests that philosophers should not accept doctrines that have hardened into dogmas even if they happen to be true, but return to the source from which the doctrine originally sprang, thinking it through afresh. But rethinking invariably modifies the inherited doctrine, and Heidegger disagrees with Aristotle on several points. Aristotle implies, despite his several categories, that the Being of genuinely existent entities is all of a piece, that everything—God, men, plants, animals, statues, and chisels—is a substance with qualities, a quantity, relations, and so on. All entities are regarded as *vorhanden*, 'present-at-hand', as appropriate objects of disinterested description.

Heidegger argues in BT that not all entities are like this. A hammer, say, is properly seen as an object of use, to be described, if at all, as 'too heavy' or 'just right', rather than in terms of its physical dimensions and properties. The token that the lover offers to the beloved is a flower, not a plant, not an object of botanical enquiry. Even philosophers who seem to distinguish between different types of entity reveal on closer inspection that they reduce the Being of these entities to a single pattern. Descartes distinguished between the *res cogitans*, the thinking thing or substance, and the *res extensa*, the extended thing or substance. But not only does he thereby equate the Being of tools and that of planets, both being at bottom simply extended things; he also, if less obviously, assimilates the Being of the thinking thing with that of the extended thing, for each is a thing with an essential attribute, albeit a different attribute. Might we say that everything that is or exists does so in the same way, that to exist is to be a bearer of predicates (or 'the value of a variable'), and that entities that apparently *are* in different ways simply bear different predicates? But not everything, Heidegger replies, is a bearer of predicates; to assume that it is introduces a surreptitious homogenization of being.

Why do philosophers homogenize the Being of entities? One reason is that they focus on entities to the exclusion of the context in which they lie. It is easier to see a hammer as *vorhanden*, as a thing with certain properties or predicates, if one ignores the engrossed carpenter hammering in a nail. We should consider not simply the Being of entities within the world, but the Being of their surrounding context, and ultimately the Being of the world as a whole. We should also look at Being as such, to see how and why it branches out into different varieties.

Heidegger does not, however, immediately consider either beings as a whole or Being as such. He turns to the examination of the human being, Dasein.

Chapter 4
Dasein

Philosophers often have reason to place the human being at the centre of their enquiry. An epistemologist who asks 'What can I know?' can be expected to discuss the status of the knower. For a phenomenologist such as Husserl, exploring the relationship between, on the one hand, the 'transcendental' ego, subject, or consciousness and, on the other, its objects, the human being is central. (Heidegger often criticizes these philosophers for saying too little about the Being of the subject.)

But if we are concerned about Being and beings, the human being seems to have no privileged status. It is simply one being among others. Why should we start with any particular entity, and why Dasein in particular? Aristotle himself held that the study of Being must begin with an exemplary type of being, namely substance, and with the exemplary instance of that type, namely God. But Heidegger rejected the link between ontology and theology that Aristotle thereby established, and does not suggest explicitly that Dasein is an exemplary or paradigmatic entity. What he says is that it is Dasein that asks the question 'What is Being?'

But, we interject, any question whatsoever is asked by Dasein. Are we to suppose that to answer, say, the question 'What are the mating habits of giraffes?' we need first to explore the Being of the human being who asks the question? In a sense we do. For to ask and to set about answering any question we need a preliminary understanding, however vague, of the subject matter of the question and of the direction in which the answer is to be sought. We need to know that the meaning of the word 'giraffe' is to be found in a dictionary or encyclopaedia, and we are likely to know even more than that if the question arouses our interest. Our preliminary understanding of giraffes is, however, not a subject of great interest nor is it, after it has given us initial guidance, of much relevance to our question.

Likewise Dasein has a preliminary understanding of Being. Without it we could not understand the question 'What is Being?' nor set about answering it. All human beings, even those who do not ask this question, have some understanding of Being, otherwise they could not engage with beings, even with themselves. (Heidegger does not consider infants in his published works, but he would doubtless say firstly that an infant capable of learning by interacting with entities must already have some implicit understanding of being, and secondly that we only understand infancy as a 'privation' of adulthood, by contrast with our understanding of full-fledged Dasein.)

Such understanding is not an explicit conceptual account of Being, nor need it be wholly impeccable. It is prone to various types of error. But we cannot, as in the case of giraffes, abandon our preliminary understanding, after initially consulting it, in search of the real object of our quest, hoping to correct any errors by confronting Being face to face. For the Being of beings is not as localized, conspicuous, or independent of ourselves as the mating habits of giraffes. Being is everywhere: everything is—people, hammers, towns, theories, planets, galaxies. Being is nowhere: it does not inhere in entities as a readily discernible property; to discern it, we need continuous guidance from our preliminary understanding of Being, and, whatever adjustments we may make, we can never wholly abandon it for, or test it against, a stark encounter with Being itself.

The Being of beings, of other entities as well as of Dasein itself, is not independent of Dasein: theories, questions, tools, cities—all these depend for their existence and their mode of Being, on the fact that they are produced, asked, used, inhabited, and interpreted by humans. Dasein is essentially in the world: it not only occupies a place in the world together with other things, but continually interprets and engages with other entities and the context in which they lie, the 'environment' or the 'world around us'. It is only because Dasein does this that there is a unitary world at all rather than a collection of entities. Dasein is not just one thing among others; it is at the centre of the world, drawing together its threads. In selecting Dasein as the starting point for his enquiry Heidegger does not focus on one type of entity to the exclusion of others; Dasein brings the whole world along with it.

Why 'Dasein'?

'Dasein' is Heidegger's way of referring both to the human being and to the type of Being that humans have. It comes from the verb *dasein*, 'to exist' or 'to be there, to be here'. The noun *Dasein* is used by other philosophers, such as Kant, for the existence of any entity. But Heidegger restricts it to humans. He stresses the root meaning of the noun, 'being there' or 'being here'. *Da* in ordinary German sometimes amounts to 'there' ('There they go'), sometimes to 'here' ('Here they come'). (Heidegger occasionally suggests that while 'here' (*hier*) is where I, the speaker, am, and 'there' (*dort*) is where he or she, the person spoken about, is, *da* is where you, the addressee of my remarks, are (xx. 343). But he does not usually regard Dasein as you rather than me.) The word *sein* means 'to be' and, as a noun (*Sein*), 'Being' in the abstract sense. Sometimes, but not always, Heidegger hyphenates the word, '*Da-sein*', to stress the sense of 'being (t)here'.

Why speak of human beings in this way? Our Being is strikingly different from that of other entities. 'Dasein is an entity for which, in its Being, that Being is an issue' (BT, 191). Unlike other entities, we have no definite essence:

> The essence of Dasein lies in its existence. Accordingly those characteristics which can be exhibited in this entity are not 'properties' present-at-hand of some entity which 'looks' so and so and is itself present-at-hand; they are in each case possible ways for it to be, and no more than that.... So when we designate this entity with the term 'Dasein', we are expressing not its 'what' (as if it were a table, house, or tree) but its Being.
>
> (BT, 42)

That Dasein's Being is an issue for it depends, in part, on the fact that this Being is 'in each case mine', that Dasein needs to be addressed with a personal pronoun, 'I' or 'you'. The Being of entities that are merely present-at-hand and are not therefore appropriately addressed as 'I' or 'you' is a matter of indifference to them. Since they cannot take charge of their own Being, they need, if they are to be anything at all, a definite 'what'. But a human being is whatever it decides to be: 'Dasein is its possibility' (BT, 42). Dasein violates Aristotle's ontology in two respects. Firstly, it is not a substance with an essential nature and properties or 'accidents'. Secondly, Dasein's potentiality or possibility is prior to its actuality: Dasein is not a definite actual thing, but the possibility of various ways of Being.

'To be or not to be, that is the question'

We naturally think of Hamlet. Dasein is an entity that can decide whether to be or not. But Hamlet does not suggest that a human is nothing more than something that can decide whether or not to be. Why might it not also have, like 'a table, house, or tree', some determinate nature? It must have some further characteristic apart from this ability to decide whether or not to be. Nothing could consist solely in that capacity, any more than it could have existence as its sole characteristic. Moreover, a human does not have an unrestricted power to decide whether or not to be. It may choose to die, but it cannot choose to be born, or to be born in one situation rather than another. It is, as Heidegger says, 'thrown' or cast into the world. But once Dasein is thrown it has more control over its own Being than just the option of suicide if it does not like what it is. (Heidegger does not mention suicide in BT, but in xx. 439 he regards it as an inappropriate or 'inauthentic' response to the possibility of death.) What I decide is not so much whether or not to be, but how to be. Here we have a different use of expressions such as 'how it is', and 'manner, mode, or way of Being'.

So far we have assumed that an entity has one, and only one, way of Being, but now we see that Dasein's way of Being involves the capacity to choose among several possible ways of Being. I can choose to be a priest, a doctor, or a philosopher. An appropriate answer to the question 'What am I?' takes the form not of a disinterested comment on myself, but of a decision about how I am to be, even if it is only the confirmation of a decision I have already made. Heidegger marks this special character by saying that Dasein, alone of all entities, *exists* or has *existence*. The verb *existieren* and the noun *Existenz*, like their English equivalents, stem from Latin words meaning literally 'to stand forth' and 'standing forth'. Dasein stands forth, creating its own ways of Being, in a way that no other entity does. This feature of Dasein is so crucial that instead of speaking of 'categories', as we do in the case of other entities, Heidegger speaks of 'existentials' (*Existenzialien*), to mark the basic features of Dasein's Being (BT, 44).

Is it not an exaggeration to say that Dasein involves no 'what', no 'properties', but consists wholly in its 'possibility'? I may be too stupid to become a priest, a doctor, or a philosopher. I may become bald, through no choice of my own and with no possibility of regrowing my hair. Most humans have a biological structure which differs markedly from that of other creatures and they have only limited possibilities of altering it. Some philosophers have located man's distinctive nature in rationality, defining man as a rational animal. Heidegger rejects this, but he does not claim that Dasein can become whatever it wants. Circumstances restrict my options: 'Existentiality is always determined by facticity' (BT, 192). But my circumstances are never simply 'present-at-hand properties': I can always respond in various ways. If I become bald, I may refuse to accept that I am bald, continuing to insist that I have a full head of hair; I may wallow in my baldness, and let it drive me to despair; I may wear a wig; I may simply ignore it; or I may gladly accept my baldness, flaunt it, and perhaps make it the basis of a career as a lover or an actor. Which option I take is not determined solely by my baldness, but is freely chosen by me.

Inauthenticity and the 'they'

But is it freely chosen by me? The fact that baldness is a significant feature of a person requiring some special response depends on social conventions that I did not initiate, and so too does the range of appropriate responses. Wearing a wig is an acceptable response, whereas shaving the heads of everyone else so that I am no longer exceptional is not. 'One does not do such things', I think, and I exclude this as an option, to such an extent that I am unlikely even to consider the possibility. Insofar as I neglect or reject certain options for the reason that 'they', 'one', or 'we' do not do such things, my condition is one of 'inauthenticity' rather than 'authenticity', and I have ceded my decision to 'others' or to the anonymous 'they'.

Heidegger's word for 'authentic' is *eigentlich*, which ordinarily means 'real' or 'proper'. From it he forms *Eigentlichkeit*, 'authenticity'. 'Inauthentic' is *uneigentlich*, which usually means 'not literal, figurative', and 'inauthenticity' is *Uneigentlichkeit*. Dasein is sometimes authentic and sometimes not. Does Heidegger mean that only authentic Dasein is really human, while inauthentic Dasein is not? No. He associates *eigentlich* with the adjective *eigen*, 'own', used in such contexts as 'having a room of one's own', 'having a mind of one's own', and 'being one's own master'. To be authentic is to be true to one's *own* self, to be one's *own* person, to do one's *own* thing.

Whose mind might I have, whose person might I be, if not my own? 'Own' usually contrasts with '(an)other's', and *eigen* contrasts with *fremd*, 'alien, another's'. I might emulate some other person or group—Heidegger, my spouse, or my academic colleagues—doing and thinking what they do and think. But more often, Heidegger believes, I conform to what the '*they*' does and thinks. He exploits a simple German pronoun, *man*, 'one', as in 'One pays one's debts', though English often uses 'we', 'they', 'you', or 'people' where German uses *man*. Heidegger turns this pronoun into a definite noun, *das Man*, the 'one' or the 'they'. The 'they' is others, but it also includes myself insofar as I do, think, and feel what 'they' do, think, and feel. It is not definite named others, it is everyone and no one. I am writing in English, because that is what *one* does. I grieve at funerals because that is what *one* does. Insofar as I conform to the 'they', I am not my own individual self, but the *they-self*: 'The Self of everyday Dasein is the they-self, which we distinguish from the *authentic Self*' (BT, 129). Dasein is inauthentic insofar as it does things simply because that is what *one* does. It is authentic insofar as it makes up its own mind, is its own person, or is true to its own self. Authenticity need not imply eccentricity. Eccentricity can be inauthentic, while conformity to standard practices can be authentically chosen. (There are two ways of being enslaved to public opinion: being afraid to disagree with it and being afraid to agree with it.)

Inauthenticity is no unqualified blemish. It is the normal condition of most of us for most of the time, and without it we could not make decisions at all. I could not decide to write a book, had I not acquired a language such as English. Then, given that my intended audience is anglophone, it does not occur to me to wonder whether I should write in ancient Greek, whether to write from left to right or from right to left, or whether to use the word 'good' in the sense of 'bad'. Conversely, the fact that I am bound to write in English does not commit me to repeating sentences and phrases used by others, 'clichés' and stock expressions; if I do this, without working out my own ideas or finding an apt, if hitherto unused, expression for them, my inauthenticity is out of place.

Still, whether my inauthenticity is appropriate or not, the question arises: can I, insofar as I am inauthentic, be said to decide my own Being? Heidegger's answer is that if I am inauthentic, if I have ceded my decisions to the 'they', I have, implicitly, decided to do so. It is always possible for me to reclaim my choice; it may not be easy, but it is at least possible. So if I can by my decision escape from inauthenticity, my failure to do so depends on a decision, however implicit, not to make my escape. Dasein's inauthenticity then does not mean that Dasein does not 'exist', dispose, that is, over its own Being.

Dasein and the body

What about the body? Is that not a definite, inescapable 'what' that every human possesses? My body is not only a 'what': I can decide to do many things both with it and to it. But any human being must be embodied and there is a central biological core that cannot be removed or radically altered.

It is clear from Heidegger's account that Dasein is embodied, not a bare ego or an exclusively psychological subject. But he rarely mentions the body. Suppose then that I attempt to describe the human body. How am I to do it? I might try to describe it in terms which do not essentially imply that it is the body of a living person who walks, talks, hammers, and so on, in terms that liken it to a corpse or to the bodies of other animals. But then, Heidegger objects, if we regard the body in this way, we have to add something to it to make up the complete human being as distinct from a corpse or an animal—a soul, say, or rationality—and then we have lost the unity of the human being, and still need to explain how this unity arises. Again, to regard one's own body in this way is a sophisticated and unnatural procedure. We do not become aware of ourselves, or others, first as extended bodies on a par with stones and rocks, then as living organisms, then as animal bodies, and finally as human beings. We start off, in adulthood, viewing ourselves as whole human beings, and need a special sort of abstraction to see ourselves simply as animals or as bodies.

The philosopher too, then, should begin by considering Dasein rather than its body, the whole human being who asks the question 'What is my body?' as it asks the question 'What is Being?' When we turn to Dasein, however, we see that we do not normally notice or attend to our own bodies when they are in good working order. G. E. Moore once held up his hands and declared 'I know I have two hands', but we do not usually make such claims about our hands or focus on them at all. We attend to the task in hand, the pen rather than the hand that holds it, or more likely the paper on which we are writing, or more likely still the matters we are writing about.

The body is inconspicuous. It is there, but it lies in the background of Dasein's doings, not in the foreground. It is not something added to Dasein, or to which Dasein is added. Dasein essentially requires a body of a certain sort, and is not a soul or ego that might conceivably exist in a disembodied state or in a body quite different from the typical human body. Dasein, its nature and capacities—the software—is intimately intertwined with its hardware, the body. Nevertheless the software is for Heidegger primary and the hardware secondary.

Dasein and spirit

Heidegger has good reason for beginning with human beings as Dasein, as questioners, choosers, and self-producers; that is where we all start from, whether we are biologists, historians, or craftsmen. Yet Dasein is only one aspect of human beings alongside others, not only biology, but also psychology and what German philosophers often call 'spirit' (*Geist*) or the 'spiritual'—sciences, theories, works of art, even our social and political structures.

Does Heidegger neglect all this? No. They all come in, but only as ways of Dasein's Being. Heidegger acknowledges no purely inner psychological realm, nor any ideal realm of logical and mathematical entities. His talk of Dasein's 'Being' involves a sturdy realism that demotes, if it does not abolish, such disciplines as logic, psychology, and epistemology. Dasein, even in its deepest moods and emotions, is always engaged with the world and with entities in it. Scientific theories, even the truths of logic and mathematics, are ways of Dasein's Being, of its Being-in-the-world.

Chapter 5
The world

Heidegger begins by considering Dasein in its 'average everydayness'. Not all of Dasein's capacities are exerted in average everydayness. It does not make momentous decisions or, usually, contemplate its own death. Above all, it does not reflect conceptually on its own condition as philosophers do. To account for his own ability to do philosophy, even to the extent of reflecting on the everyday condition, Heidegger must go beyond average everydayness. But the philosopher is also a human being and, like the rest of humanity, spends much of his time in everydayness. It would be a serious error to describe Dasein as if it were unremittingly engaged in philosophical enquiry. Yet Dasein in average everydayness shares many characteristics with Dasein in more elevated modes.

Dasein, whether in average everydayness or otherwise, is in the world. Stones, trees, cows, and hammers are also in the world. Dasein too is in the world in the way they are. But Dasein is also in the world in a sense in which other entities are not. Dasein, unlike a stone, a tree, or even a cow, is aware of and familiar with the world, aware of other things in the world and of itself, and is so in virtue of its 'understanding of Being'. It is not a self-enclosed subject, aware only of its own mental states. If it were so, it would have a definite 'what' and would neither be, nor need to be, in the world. If Dasein had a determinate nature of its own and

31

were not, at least in part, what it makes of itself, it might not need a world to dwell in. But as things are, Dasein, to be at all, at least in its own characteristic ways, needs a world populated with entities to engage with.

What is Dasein's world like? It is not primarily a world of purely natural entities. The most immediate and obvious denizens of Dasein's world, apart from itself, are the tools and equipment for its daily needs, its hammer, say, and the nails and the leather for making shoes. Tools and equipment have their place in a workshop, the immediate environing world of Dasein. But this world points beyond to a larger world, to the other Dasein who buy shoes, and those who supply leather. This in turn points to nature—not the nature of scientists, but the cows from which leather comes and the fields in which they graze. Husserl called this world, in which we naturally and normally live, the *Lebenswelt* or 'life-world'. Heidegger simply called it the world (*Welt*), the wider world beyond the immediate 'world around us' (*Umwelt*), the world of the workplace.

Philosophers have often neglected the world in this sense, assuming that the world we inhabit consists of extended natural entities. Descartes, in his *Meditations on First Philosophy*, doubts the reality of the life-world, the fire before him, the cloak wrapped around him, the pen in his hand, and paper on his lap. When later in the work he overcomes doubt and restores his belief in the external world, it is the world of mathematical physics, of measurable extended things that wins his assent, not the humble *Umwelt* of the fire, the cloak, the pen, and paper.

But even philosophers who try to give the life-world its due tend to misdescribe it. A phenomenologist such as Husserl, 'abstracting at first from all "significance" predicates and restricting himself purely to the "res extensa"' (CM, 47), describes the experience of seeing a table in the following way. As I walk round a table, it presents to me various visual aspects which, though not identical in shape and colour, are systematically related to each other in such a way that I can, by 'retaining' or remembering the aspects of the table that I have already seen, eventually 'synthesize' them or piece them together to form a conception of the table as it objectively is, a brown rectangular top based on four legs. Heidegger gives, in early Freiburg lectures on ontology (lxiii. 88–92), a different account. What I see is not just *a* table, but *the* table, the table in *this* room. The table is for writing on, or for eating at. I see it as *for* something. I do not first see it as an extended object and only later as for something. I hardly notice its geometrical dimensions or its spatial location with respect to the points of the compass. I see it as well or badly positioned, as, say, too far from the light for reading. I notice scratches on the table, not just interruptions of its uniform colour, but damage done by the children. I think back to the past and recall that it is the table at which we used to discuss politics or at which I wrote my first book.

In this account Heidegger is contemplating a segment of the world, not actively engaging with it like the craftsman at work. But the two situations exhibit important similarities, as well as differences. Firstly, theoretical cognition is not primarily or even necessarily involved at all. The craftsman does not regard his hammer, and Heidegger does not view the table, as an entity with certain geometrical and physical properties. Both are seen primarily as objects of use, connected to human purposes: the hammer is for hammering, the table is for eating or writing.

Secondly, neither the hammer nor the table is seen in isolation from other entities in the setting. The hammer is for hammering in the nails that lie next to it, for working the leather into shoes, and so on. The table is too far from the window, it is where the people I hear outside usually eat, it is where I wrote that book on the shelf. Different entities in the room or the workshop refer to each other, and thereby form a significant whole—a complete workshop or room—rather than a random collection of entities.

33

Objects refer to each other in these ways and thus constitute a realm of 'significance' most obviously and easily if they are objects of use—'ready-to-hand', *zuhanden*, in contrast to entities that are merely 'present-at-hand', *vorhanden*. Neither the workshop nor the room is a self-enclosed environment. The workshop and its contents refer beyond to customers, cows, and meadows. The room too refers to the carpenter who made the table, the tradesmen who supply food, the publishers who print books, and so on. The immediate world around us points to a larger world beyond, but a world still anchored in Dasein, its needs and purposes.

Thirdly, space and time are involved in both situations, but with a different role from that assigned to them by Husserl. Husserl is interested primarily in geometrical shapes, the shapes both of the different perspectival aspects of the table that successively present themselves, and of the actual table that we piece together from these aspects. Time for Husserl is primarily our temporal awareness of our experiences of the table. When I first see a table, I experience not the table as a whole but an aspect of it from a particular standpoint. If I have seen a table before, I expect or anticipate that my experiences as I walk round the table will be of a certain sort, I 'protain' my subsequent experiences. As I continue to walk around it, these expectations or 'protentions' are 'fulfilled' by actual experiences. But this would be of little benefit if I at once forgot the experiences I had already had, if I did not 'retain' my past experiences as well as have my present one and protain those to come. Retention and protention enable me to be aware of the temporal flow of my experiences and to view them as experiences of an objective table, whose actual shape does not correspond exactly to any single experience of it.

For Heidegger, impressed though he was by Husserl's analyses, space and time play a different role. What we naturally notice about the table is not its precise shape and dimensions, but whether it is the right size and in the right place for our purposes.

Is it big enough to seat the whole family for a meal? Is it too far from the light or from the bookcase for writing? Objects have their proper positions in the room. So too in the workshop. Nails, leather, and hammer are placed within easy reach on the workbench. Through the window the craftsman can see the road that leads, in one direction, to the centre of the town and, in the other, to the next village, where his sister now lives. He does not know the exact distances to these places, but he knows that it is only a short walk to the town centre, while the walk to the next village takes some time and he is usually hungry by the time he gets there. (German peasants often expressed the distance from one place to another, and the time needed to traverse it, by the number of pipefuls one would smoke on the journey.) Time too is a matter of 'significance'. The table points ahead to the uses that will be made of it, and back to past events—the scratches made by the boys, the book he wrote at it, and so on. The craftsman too, absorbed in his hammering, looks ahead implicitly to the shoe he will have made, to the fresh supply of leather he needs to order, and back perhaps to his youth when he was taught his skills by his father, from whom he inherited the workshop.

There is, however, an important difference between these two situations. As Heidegger surveys the room he notices the scratches on the table, he explicitly recalls eating, writing, and conversing at the table, and so on. But the craftsman, engrossed in hammering a nail, does not explicitly notice or attend to the bench he is working on, the stool he sits on, the supply of nails beside him. He need not be thinking about his customers, his suppliers, the cows in the meadow. These things are *there* for him, he is tacitly aware of them, but they are inconspicuous and unobtrusive; he sees them out of the corner of his eye and does not focus on them. This is possible because these entities refer to each other and constitute a web of significance. The stool, the bench, the nails beside him, even the hammer itself, remain inconspicuous as long as they are in their proper positions, ready to play their part in his task. He will notice them if something goes wrong. If the head of the hammer comes off or the stool collapses they become conspicuous. Or, again, if his leather is missing, runs out, or is not in its proper place, it becomes conspicuous in a way that it was not before.

The same is true of the craftsman himself. Husserl was mistaken to say that the 'ego is himself existent for himself in continuous evidence' (CM, 66). When the craftsman is absorbed in his work, he focuses on the nail he is hammering or the shoe he is making. He is barely aware of himself even as an embodied agent, let alone as an 'ego'. He may focus on himself if something goes wrong, but he is otherwise as inconspicuous to himself as the nails beside him or the spectacles on his nose. It has been a persistent mistake of past philosophers to make things too conspicuous: 'when direction on an object is taken as the basic structure of consciousness, Being in the world is characterized far too explicitly and sharply' (xvii. 318).

The world and things within the world are normally inconspicuous to everyday Dasein. This raises a problem. Philosophers are not a distinct species from everyday Dasein. How then can they rise above average everydayness to become aware of what everyday Dasein fails to notice? Heidegger regards himself as a phenomenologist in the sense that he makes apparent what is usually inconspicuous, and he does not do so by out-of-the-way experiments or abstruse arguments. What Heidegger notices, and presents in conceptual garb, is obvious to anyone once it is pointed out. But how does he notice it in the first place? Conversely, we may think that what Heidegger has pointed out is radiantly obvious and that the mystery is that any philosopher ever overlooked it. Heidegger has a complex task: he has not only to give an analysis of Dasein and to convince us of its correctness, he has also to explain why he—unlike everyday Dasein—is able to give this account and also why other philosophers, not themselves perpetually enmeshed in everydayness, were not.

Being-in-the-world

Dasein and the world are not two distinct things that can vary independently of each other. They are complementary. If we regard either in a certain way, this will commit us to regarding the other in a certain way or at least exclude certain ways of viewing it. If we regard the world in Descartes's way, as a collection of extended things, then it is natural to view the self as a thinking thing; conversely, if we view the self as a thinking thing it is natural to view the world it inhabits as consisting of present-at-hand extended things. If we reject this account and view the world as a web of significance, then we are committed to a different view of Dasein.

Dasein's approach to the things around it is a practical one of circumspect concern rather than disinterested contemplation. Heidegger does not deny that there are derelict craftsmen who neglect their affairs or that a usually industrious craftsman may have a headache today and feel that he cannot be bothered. Even what we normally regard as a lack of concern is a sort of concern—Dasein never lacks concern in the way that a stone, a tree, or a cow does. But Dasein's attitude is not only practical. The customary distinction between the practical and the theoretical, action and knowledge, is a construct that lies above the level of everyday Dasein. Dasein also knows things. It knows what a hammer is for; it knows how to use it; it knows where the leather is kept; it knows its way around the workshop. It cannot say how it knows all this or put its knowledge into words, but it knows as well as does things. If it did not, there could not be a world in Heidegger's sense. Tools that nobody knows how to use, or ever knew how to use, cannot constitute a web of interreferential significance; they would lie indifferently alongside each other like rocks in an uninhabited desert.

Dasein knows not only the individual items in the workshop and how to use them. It also knows the world and knows its way about

in it. What Heidegger has in mind is best illustrated by the sense
of direction that enables us to find our way around a familiar
town. We cannot easily say how we do it or give explicit directions
to a stranger, but we manage to find our own way without
difficulty. We do not painfully pick our way along a familiar route
by noting the houses and side-streets on the way; we walk straight
to our destination, often oblivious of our surroundings along the
way. Usually we do it without maps. A map would be of little use
to someone who lacked altogether a sense of direction; we need a
sense of direction even to find our way around the map and then
orient the map to our environment.

Nor is this just an analogy. For Dasein's world is, Heidegger
stresses, a spatial world. It is not spatial in the way that Descartes's
and Newton's (or even Leibniz's) world is spatial, a world of cold,
neutral coordinates. It is a world of directions—up–down, left–right,
behind–ahead, and north–south–east–west. It is a world where
things are near and far, but distances are not measured only in
miles or kilometres; what is near as the crow flies may be far if an
unbridged river or a trackless mountain lies between, and things
that are too close may, like one's spectacles, be too near to be seen.
It is a world in which things have their rightful places, not a purely
Euclidean world in which an object may occupy any place of the
appropriate size.

The a priori

How is such Being-in-the-world possible? Is Dasein simply a
blank tablet that takes on whatever the world offers to it? Not in
Heidegger's view. Since the world and Dasein are complementary,
features of the world are to be explained in terms of features of
Dasein, and the most basic of these features are a priori.

Much of what Dasein knows is learned fairly late in its career. One
Dasein can handle a word processor and find its way around the
keyboard, but knows little about cricket or the details of a

cobbler's workshop. Another knows about cricket or shoemaking, but nothing about word processors. But we all know, however tacitly and implicitly, about tools and equipment, and what an 'equipmental context' is, what a cricket pitch, a cobbler's workshop, and a writer's study have in common. Even someone from a quite different culture, entirely unfamiliar with our practices and occupations, would if he were transported into our world recognize what he saw as a workshop, and not a mere jumble of entities, even if he knew nothing about the details (xx. 334). Understanding what a tool is, and what a world is in which tools lie, is a part of Dasein's essential understanding of Being without which it would not be Dasein.

Or take, again, spatiality. Dasein does not simply read off its sense of direction from the world around it. The world is spatial because Dasein is spatial. A Dasein that finds its way easily round Messkirch or Freiburg cannot immediately transfer its skill to Marburg, Berlin, Los Angeles, or the Gobi Desert. If transferred to any of these places it will feel disoriented; even though it recognizes individual buildings, streets, or mounds, it cannot find its bearings. But its being disoriented is a mark of its intrinsic spatiality, and soon it will come to orient itself, seeing its new environment in terms of the familiar spatial directions.

Being-with-others

Heidegger gives a similar account of our relations with other people. Philosophers, especially though not exclusively those who, like Husserl, regard a human being as primarily acquainted with its own mental states, present our awareness of others in the following way. First, I become aware of my own existence and of other non-human entities. I get to know the shape, appearance, and doings of my own body and I am also aware of the inner experiences I have. Then I notice that there are other entities of a similar appearance to myself who behave in broadly similar ways when subjected to similar stimuli. The philosopher then wonders how it is possible—intelligible and justifiable—for me to attribute to these beings inner mental states similar to my own. Is it by empathy? How is empathy possible?

This approach is mistaken. It ignores both Dasein's understanding of Being and its Being-in-the-world. As long as it exists Dasein is 'with others'. It knows what another person is as well as it knows itself, or any other entity. It does not need to inspect the details of a person's physique to discover that it is a person; we are often aware of the presence of others, of what they are doing and of their attitude towards us, while unaware of the details of their appearance. Even when there are no other people around—the workshop is empty, or the desert is uninhabited—others are conspicuous by their absence: 'Even Dasein's being alone is Being-with in the world' (xx. 328).

Heidegger is not simply describing the phenomenal character of our experience of others. He is describing a structural feature of Dasein. Dasein alone is incomplete, it has no nature of its own in which to bask, but has to decide how to be. Then virtually everything Dasein does or is cries out for others, as suppliers of its raw materials, as purchasers of its products, as hearers, or as readers. Dasein's world is essentially a public world, accessible to others as well as itself.

Moods

Heidegger does not speak of 'knowledge' in such cases. The term 'knowledge' suggests something too explicit and theoretical. He speaks rather of 'understanding'—understanding how to do things, the world, other people, and, in general, understanding of Being. But before explaining what understanding is, he turns to *moods*.

Moods are often regarded as mental things, inner feelings that play only a subdued role in our engagement with the world. But that is not how Heidegger sees them. To be in a certain mood is to view the world in a certain way, and it crucially affects our engagement with the world and our response to entities within it.

Moods differ from emotions. Emotions concern particular entities—I am angry about something and usually with someone—but if I am in an irritable mood, I need not be irritable about anything in particular, though I am more likely to get angry about particular things than I usually do. If moods are directed at anything they are directed at the world rather than at entities within it. Anxiety, objectless *Angst*, or boredom (to take Heidegger's examples) cast a pall over the world, in contrast to fear in the face of a specific threat or boredom with something specific, such as the minister's speech.

Moods are hardly within our control. I can control my deeds, decide what to do, and restrain myself from doing what I have an urge to do. To a degree I can control my emotions: I can refrain from insulting the object of my anger, and turn my thoughts to something else to alleviate my anger. But moods come and go as they please, unresponsive to our direction.

Since they do not concern specific entities, I cannot remove the pall of depression by manipulating specific entities; everything to which I turn my attention lies under the same pall. Heidegger expresses this with an unusual word, *Befindlichkeit*, which means roughly 'how one finds oneself', 'how one is to be found', or 'how one is doing', but is often misleadingly translated as 'state of mind'. The usual word for mood, *Stimmung*, also means the 'tuning' of a musical instrument, and Heidegger exploits this association: to be in a mood is to be tuned or attuned in a certain way.

Are moods as significant as Heidegger supposes? Most of us, for most of the time, are in no definable mood, and even in a bad mood we go about our normal business in much the same way as when in a good mood. But what is our normal business? Why is Heidegger looking at the table and the room in which it lies rather than getting down to business, as the craftsman does in his workshop? Is it because he is alone in the house? No. There may be people in the next room engaged in a heated conversation or a game of cards. Even if he is alone, he could take the opportunity to read a book or draft a plan for writing one. Is it that he understands more or less than the others do about his surroundings? No. The craftsman and others in the house understand as much as Heidegger does. They too sometimes survey their surroundings, though they do not describe them as aptly as Heidegger does. It must be because Heidegger is in a mood of, say, pensive nostalgia. He is not in the mood for conversation, cards, reading, or writing. He may be snapped out of his present mood if the others cajole him, or he may steel himself to engage in these activities in the face of his mood. But not all moods are so easily dispelled:

> I walked to a neighbouring town; and sat down upon a settle in the street, and fell into a very deep pause about the most fearful state my sin had brought me to; and, after long musing, I lifted up my head; but methought I saw as if the sun that shineth in the heavens did grudge to give me light; and as if the very stones in the street, and tiles upon the houses, did band themselves against me. Me thought that they all combined together to banish me out of the world. I was abhorred of them, and unfit to dwell among them, because I had sinned against the Saviour. Oh, how happy now was every creature over I for they stood fast, and kept their station. But I was gone and lost.

> John Bunyan, *Grace Abounding*

Few of us are in such a disabling mood for long. Can we not ignore such unusual moods as peripheral to Being-in-the-world? Even if we could, it would not follow that moods as such are unimportant. For if the busy craftsman or the pensive Heidegger are not, and cannot be, in such a mood as Bunyan describes, they must be in some other mood. Dasein is never moodless, any more than it is ever unconcerned. To be in the average, everyday, apparently moodless condition is itself to be in a mood, albeit a mood for which we have only a brief description. The music that is often essential for disclosing the world of a film conveys the *mood* of the film—contentment, excitement, anxious expectancy, or average everydayness. But it is only in films that moods need music. We bring our own moods to the world without special aids.

Is Bunyan's mood really disabling? While it lasts it prevents him from making shoes, writing books, engaging in either the humdrum routine of life or in making crucial decisions. It is not an appropriate response to any sin that most of us, least of all Bunyan himself, have committed. Most of us are glad to be free of such moods. But most of us are not philosophers of Heidegger's stature and dedication. For moods such as this reveal things that we are usually unaware of. They light up the world and our Being-in-the-world in a way that everyday business does not. The craftsman catches a glimpse of his world, of the worldly character of his world, when he finds a tool missing; he notices the whole in the conspicuously absent part. But a mood such as Bunyan's discloses the world more forcibly and memorably: it reveals the worldliness of the world and, by contrast, the everyday unobtrusiveness of the world. Such moods, even less extreme cases such as boredom and *Angst*, are a vital source of insight for the philosopher. But they are not the exclusive preserve of the philosopher. Unphilosophical, everyday Dasein is prone to them too, so moods play a part in Heidegger's attempt to explain how Dasein becomes a philosopher.

Moods alone, however, do not disclose the world. For this we need understanding.

Understanding

Everyday Dasein understands the world, things in the world, and itself. Here again we see a connexion between everyday Dasein and the philosopher. For Heidegger too wants to understand and interpret Dasein, the world, and their Being. (The Introduction to BT speaks of his enterprise as hermeneutic, interpretative—somewhat like, though not exactly like, the interpretation of a text.) Heidegger's enterprise is a continuation of what Dasein does every day, but it is not simply a continuation of it. For Heidegger wants to give a conceptual account of what he understands, while everyday Dasein understands only preconceptually. Its understanding is not theoretical cognition. Cognition presupposes a prior understanding of what we wish to know, in much the way that Heidegger's conceptual account of the meaning of Being presupposes a prior *understanding* of being. Understanding does not stand in contrast to other approaches to things, such as knowing about them or explaining them. It is presupposed by them all, since it in part constitutes our Being-in-the-world.

What Dasein understands is not so much any particular item in its environment, as its environment as a whole and its own place in it. But Dasein does not simply understand its environment as one might understand an alien text or culture from which one is entirely disengaged. It understands it as presenting to it a range of possibilities. If it did not understand it in this way it could not understand its environment as 'significant'.

Although Heidegger speaks of understanding's 'projection' of Dasein on its possibilities, he has in mind nothing so definite and deliberate as a 'project' or plan, but simply that 'as long as it is, Dasein always has understood itself and always will understand itself in terms of possibilities' (BT, 145). The shoemaker sees his workshop as a field of possibilities for him, and is perhaps wondering what to do next. Even the carefree sunbather understands himself in terms of the possibilities of continuing to lie where he is, taking a dip in the sea, or refilling his glass. Dasein is 'constantly more than it factually is' (BT, 145), always poised between alternative possible ways of continuing. (Even in sleep we are dispositionally geared up for tomorrow's business, as we are dispositionally still in the world.) We are not passive creatures, roused to activity only by external stimuli; we are constantly up to something.

Interpretation

More explicit than understanding is interpretation, which in German (*Auslegung*) also means 'laying out'. What I interpret is not so much my environment as a whole, but specific items within it, and also myself. I interpret something as a hammer, say, and I do so primarily in terms of what it is for, such as banging in nails. Although interpretation does not focus on the environment as a whole, it presupposes an understanding of it. I cannot interpret something as a hammer unless I already understand something about nails, wood, and so on. Similarly, I cannot understand something as a hammer unless I have a prior general understanding of tools and equipment. When I interpret something as a hammer I do not first see it as simply present-at-hand, as a length of wood with a piece of iron attached to it, and then interpret this as a hammer. I implicitly understand it as *zuhanden*, as equipment, from the start:

> In interpreting, we do not, so to speak, throw a 'signification' over some naked thing which is present-at-hand, we do not stick a value on it; but when something within-the-world is encountered as such, the thing in question already has an involvement which is disclosed in our understanding of the world, and this involvement is one which gets laid out by the interpretation.

> (BT, 150)

Interpretation involves a 'fore-having' (*Vorhabe*), a 'fore-sight' (*Vorsicht*), and a 'fore-conception' (*Vorgriff*) (BT, 150). The interpreter has in advance the object of his interpretation; Heidegger, for example, has a preliminary understanding of

Dasein, before he begins to interpret it. He views it in a certain way; Heidegger views Dasein with regard to its being. He has preconceptions, concepts in terms of which he proposes to interpret the object; Heidegger interprets Dasein with such concepts as 'existence'. All interpretation, from the everyday to the philosophical, involves such a 'fore-structure'.

Chapter 6
Language, truth, and care

Interpretation need not be expressed in language. I will most likely make my interpretation of something explicit, if it is broken, malfunctioning, initially unavailable, or needs to be explained to a novice. But language emerges from interpretation and the meanings or significations it lays out: 'To significations, words accrue' (BT, 161). Words and the entities they apply to are not two disparate realms: words essentially refer to entities and, conversely, entities are essentially meaning-laden and thus give rise to words.

The basic form of language is *Rede*, talk or discourse. Talk is to someone about something. It need not involve only, or indeed any, assertions; questions, orders, and so on may disclose the world as well as assertions. It need not involve grammatically complete utterances: 'Too heavy—the other one!' is perfectly good talk. Silences are as much a part of talk as are spoken sounds: someone hands me another hammer, he need not bother to explain 'No, not that one—try this instead!' Assertions emerge from talk. Instead of saying 'Too heavy—the other one!', I say 'The hammer is too heavy', and eventually 'The hammer is heavy'. Talk becomes increasingly detached from concrete speech in the workplace. A hammer is seen no longer as ready-to-hand, as a tool to be used or rejected, in its place alongside other tools, but as present-at-hand, as a bearer of properties severed from its involvements with other tools. We end up by taking such a sentence as 'Snow is white', which occurs more commonly in logic textbooks than in down-to-earth talk, as a paradigm of significant discourse. Such assertions are seen as the locus of truth. They are true if, and only if, they correspond to the facts or to some such entities within the world.

Truth

One of Heidegger's most striking doctrines is his rejection of this view of his truth. Truth, he claims, is unconcealment or uncovering. Dasein itself is the primary locus of truth: 'there is truth only insofar as Dasein is and as long as Dasein is' (BT, 227). He does not condemn or forgo assertions; they are an essential part of the philosopher's repertoire. An assertion such as 'The hammer is heavy' has three aspects (BT, 154ff.). Firstly, it points out something as a hammer and thus involves the 'as' of interpretation. But the hammer is now a present-at-hand thing, detached from its moorings in its environment. Secondly, it predicates something, heaviness, of the hammer. Thirdly, it communicates this to another. Why then are assertions not the primary locus of truth?

An assertion is true, it is suggested, if, and only if, it corresponds to a fact. This gives Heidegger two reasons for disputing the theory. If the theory is correct, there must be an assertion to correspond to a fact and a fact for it to correspond to. But neither of these items fills the role assigned to it. What, first, is an assertion? A string of words perhaps. Or a series of ideas in the mind of the speaker that is then conveyed to the hearer. Or an ideal, logical entity, a timeless proposition. But each of these types of entity—word-sounds, ideas, and propositions—are artificial constructs imposed on the primitive speech situation by a specialized view of the assertion as itself something present-at-hand; none of them naturally presents itself to the normal speaker and hearer. I do not assert something of the idea of a hammer nor does my hearer take the assertion to be about an idea. I am generally unaware of the precise words I utter, let alone the sounds I make. Nor does my hearer hear words as such; he turns to the hammer and its heaviness, and may hardly recall my exact words. Moreover, words already have meanings and thus implicitly involve the entities to which they allegedly correspond. If assertions are to be genuinely independent of the facts and capable of either corresponding to them or failing to do so, we should regard them perhaps simply as sounds. But we do not hear pure sounds:

> What we first hear is never noises or complexes of sounds, but the creaking wagon, the motor-cycle. We hear the column on the march, the north wind, the woodpecker tapping, the fire crackling. It requires a very artificial and complicated frame of mind to hear a pure noise ... Likewise, when we are explicitly hearing the discourse of another, we proximally understand what is said, or—to put it more exactly—we're already with him, in advance, alongside the entity which the discourse is about ... Even in cases where the speech is indistinct or in a foreign language, what we proximally hear is unintelligible words, and not a multiplicity of tone-data.
>
> (BT, 163f.)

Might words have meanings independent of the things they apply to, so that what corresponds to a fact is a meaningful sentence or a proposition? No. A word such as 'hammer' or 'culture' does not have a single determinate meaning or connotation; its meaning varies with the world in which it is used:

> The life of actual language consists in multiplicity of meaning. To relegate the animated, vigorous word to the immobility of a univocal, mechanically programmed sequence of signs would mean the death of language and the petrifaction and devastation of Dasein.
>
> (Ni. 144; cf. xxiv. 280f.)

There is no pre-packaged portion of meaning sufficiently independent of the world and of entities within it to correspond, or fail to correspond, to the world. Words and their meanings are already world-laden.

If we turn in the other direction and look for chunks of the world to which assertions might correspond, such as the heavy hammer, we fail to find them. The hammer is entwined in involvements with other entities and has its place in a world. All this is implicitly known to the speaker and hearer; otherwise they could not assert, hear, or understand. This world is not disclosed primarily by assertions, but by moods and understanding. Dasein then is the primary locus of truth.

Is Heidegger telling the truth?

Heidegger makes assertions. He asserts for example that assertion is not the primary locus of truth. Is that assertion, and others he makes, true? Is the theory that he rejects false? If so, in what sense are Heidegger's assertions true and those of his opponents false?

Falsity is not for Heidegger coordinate with truth, as it is for those who locate both primarily in assertions. If I assert 'The hammer is heavy' and you say 'No, the hammer is not heavy', one of us is asserting a falsehood. But for this to be possible both of us must agree that there is a hammer there and, more generally, inhabit the same world. Falsehood is only possible against a background of truth and of agreement about the truth. Nevertheless, there are falsehoods, but they do not consist in the failure of a sentence to correspond to reality. It is more a matter of covering things up, of distorting them, and this may be done in other ways than by false assertions, such as omission or non-verbal actions. (As Macaulay said: 'A history in which every particular incident may be true may on the whole be false.')

Truth consists in uncovering things, in illuminating things or shedding light on them. It is a matter of degree, of more and less, rather than of either–or. Illumination is never complete, nor ever wholly absent. (Cf. xxvi. 95: 'every philosophy, as a human thing, intrinsically fails; and God needs no philosophy'.) Thus Heidegger rarely speaks of his own views as true and those of his opponents as false. The light he casts reaches only so far, and his opponents are never, and never leave us, wholly in the dark. More often he describes his opponents' views as insufficiently 'original' or 'primordial' (*ursprünglich*), in the sense that they do not get close enough to the 'source' (*Ursprung*) or the bottom of things. Such light as they shed does not reach far enough. They may also cover things up, not only by showing things in a false light but also by casting light in the wrong direction.

Heidegger avoids condemning his opponents' views as false for another reason. Dasein is in (the) truth. Otherwise it could not be in the world. But it is also in untruth. Not only because beings have to be uncovered or illuminated by Dasein and are only ever imperfectly so, but because Dasein has an essential tendency to misinterpret both itself and other beings. A philosopher is also Dasein and is thus prone to similar misinterpretations. Philosophical mistakes are not sheer mistakes; philosophers go wrong because Dasein goes wrong. Philosophers' mistakes disclose a fundamental feature of Dasein.

Falling

Why does Dasein go wrong? Apparently for various reasons. Because Dasein is primarily engrossed in things in the world, it regards itself as a thing, as *zuhanden* or, more likely, as *vorhanden* like the things it deals with. (This is the 'ontological reflection back of world understanding onto Dasein-interpretation' (BT, 16).) Similarly, it overlooks the obvious, what is too close to be conspicuous, not only its own nature, but its own

Being-in-the-world, in contrast to the entities it deals with. Again, Dasein submits to the power of the 'they'—it does, says, feels, and thinks things simply because that is what 'they' do, say, feel, or think. Related to this is the philosopher's, but not only the philosopher's, tendency to succumb to tradition, to accept inherited concepts, doctrines, and ways of looking at things without adequate scrutiny. Heidegger groups these apparently distinct ways of going wrong under the heading of *Verfallen*, 'falling', falling away from oneself into the world.

In BT, falling is introduced by way of the further career of assertion. Assertions are essentially communicable to others. The originator of an assertion makes it in the presence of the entities that the assertion is about. But as the assertion is passed on from one person to another, it is accepted by people unfamiliar with the original evidence for it, simply because it is what 'they' say. Talk (*Rede*) becomes idle talk or chatter (*Gerede*). A close relative of chatter is curiosity, *Neugier*, which means literally 'lust for novelty'. The inquisitive chatterbox is constantly on the lookout for the latest news. One sees and reads what 'one' or 'they' has to have seen and read. Chatter and curiosity give rise to ambiguity or duplicity—the German *Zweideutigkeit* has both meanings. When everyone chatters about everything there is no way of telling who really understands what—except perhaps that someone who is really onto something does not chatter about it. Questions are presented as settled when they are really open. Ambiguity and duplicity also infects our relations with others: 'Under the mask of "for-one-another", an "against-one-another" is in play' (BT, 175). All this, and more, stems from falling:

> Dasein is proximally and for the most part alongside the 'world' of
> its concern. This 'absorption in...' has mostly the character of
> Being-lost in the publicness of the 'they'. Dasein has, in the first
> instance, always already fallen away from itself as an authentic
> ability to be its Self, and has fallen into the 'world'. 'Fallenness' into

the 'world' means an absorption in Being-with-one-another, insofar
as the latter is guided by idle talk, curiosity, and ambiguity.

(BT, 175)

To say that Dasein has fallen away from itself is not to say that it
was once in an unfallen condition. Dasein has *always already*
fallen from itself into the world in something like the way in
which I have *always already* paid income tax and never received
my gross salary (nor would I receive exactly *that* gross salary if
there were no such thing as income tax).

Heidegger's account of falling raises doubts. He now insists that
average everydayness is a state of fallenness and inauthenticity.
But can we plausibly say of the craftsman in his workshop that his
life is guided by chatter, curiosity, and ambiguity? This may be
true of the chattering classes, of consumers of culture, and of
philosophers. The honest craftsman may retail gossip about
matters beyond his expertise, be curious about his neighbours'
affairs, and make double-edged remarks to them. But none of this
is essential to the everyday pattern of his life.

Why then is falling an indispensable component of his being? For
two reasons. The craftsman is, firstly, 'proximally and for the most
part' absorbed in his daily tasks and does not, except occasionally,
step back to survey his life as a whole. Secondly, the world in
which he works is a public, not a private, world. It derives its
meaning from others, or rather from the anonymous 'they', not
from himself alone. He makes shoes of a certain type because this
is what *they* require. He makes them of leather and with a
hammer because this is how *one* makes shoes and these are among
the socially assigned uses of hammer and leather. All of this is
reasonable; there is, as far as he knows, no better way to make
shoes, and given that he is a competent cobbler with a market for
his products it would be foolish to turn his hand to another trade.
(He might use his hammer to crush a rival's skull, but this would

make him no more authentic nor elevate him out of fallenness. For murder too is a socially recognized use of a hammer, though generally disapproved of.) This is Dasein's everyday condition and it is, in Heidegger's view, but a few steps away from chatter, curiosity, and ambiguity.

What is wrong with fallenness and inauthenticity? At one level there is nothing wrong with them. They are inevitable features of the human predicament; we cannot step outside our own condition to assess it by an external standard. At another level they lead to error. Absorption in the world, or rather in worldly things, leads us to regard ourselves as present-at-hand, as a thinking thing, as a tool, machine, or computer. Our addiction to chatter leads us to detach the assertion from its anchorage in worldly significance and view it as an autonomous 'judgement'. Dasein's understanding of Being is, in these respects, an unreliable guide.

But these errors themselves are not necessarily imposed on us by the chatter of the 'they'. 'They' may say that men are machines and that assertions are 'judgements', but that is a distinct source of error. If we believe that men are machines (or 'subjects') because that is the model that most conspicuously presents itself to us in our dealings with the world, we do not need 'them' to tell it to us too. Conversely, what 'they' say may be correct. It may be ignoble and stunting simply to accept what 'they' say. It may not befit the philosopher's calling to confine his attention to the doctrines, or at least to the problems, retailed at conferences and in recent journals, but the problems may be the right ones and the solutions correct. Moreover, great past philosophers—Aristotle, Descartes, Kant—went astray too. Yet surely they were no less authentic, no less resistant to chatter and the 'they', than Heidegger himself. Heidegger seems to conflate the truth of a person's beliefs with the 'authenticity' of the person himself and of his attachment to the beliefs. He is not the first to do so. Plato too held that philosophy is not simply an effective instrument for acquiring knowledge, but a supremely valuable way of life that opens up the eye of one's soul to the truth.

Fallenness and truth

Heidegger can evade some of these charges if we recall his account of truth. Truth is uncovering and uncoveredness, shedding light and light shed. Someone who simply accepts and passes on the current chatter, even if the chatter happens to be correct, sheds no light of his own. A great philosopher, by contrast, sheds light even if his views are mistaken. His errors are likely to stem from his accepting something of the tradition without adequate inspection. But in any case the thought of great philosophers is never flatly false. It is never solidified into something simply false or simply true; it is always, as Heidegger said of himself, 'on the way', in transit, never at its destination. It always sheds enough light to guide us in the right direction, even if that leads away from the philosopher himself. Conversely, chatter is inert and self-enclosed. It 'tranquillizes' us into thinking that matters are entirely settled and disinclines us to look further.

Heidegger does not simply reject the views of his opponents. He wants to show that philosophers' errors derive from an essential feature of Dasein itself, its fallenness. He argues that everyday Dasein, exemplified by the craftsman engrossed in his work, is prone to the same failings as the philosopher, that the mistakes made by philosophers are only refined, conceptual versions of everyday misunderstandings. For example, he regards Aristotle's account of time, time as an endless sequence of 'nows' or instants, not only as the general Greek view of time, but as the 'vulgar' or 'ordinary' understanding of time: 'This ordinary way of understanding [time] has become explicit in an interpretation precipitated in the traditional concept of time, which has persisted from Aristotle to Bergson and even later' (BT, 17f.).

Why should we agree that the philosopher's concept of time or of, say, the self is already implicit in everyday Dasein's preconceptual understanding of these matters? An unphilosophical craftsman clearly does not think, in conceptual terms, that he is a thing on a par with other things or that time is a sequence of nows. These ideas have never occurred to him and he would probably not accept them immediately even if they were presented to him. Why should we say that he implicitly understands himself as a thing and time as a sequence of nows?

At one level everyday Dasein's understanding of Being must correspond closely to Heidegger's conceptual account of it. The craftsman would be unable to do his job properly and find his way around in the world, if he understood himself *exclusively* as a machine, and time *exclusively* as a sequence of nows, rather than as time *to do* things. If that were so, everyday Dasein would be wholly deluded, offering no clues to the meaning of Being or, at least, no more clues than the texts of Aristotle and Descartes.

But how could that be so? It would defy belief for Heidegger to suggest that he alone of all human beings can get Being straight when everyone else is wholly deluded. Heidegger is himself Dasein, as were Aristotle and Descartes. He needs some clue to guide him to a conceptual account of being, and if it is not to be just his own peculiar private understanding of it, which could guide him only to his own peculiar private concept of it, it must be an understanding he shares, in large measure, with others. Everyday Dasein cannot then be wholly deluded in its understanding of being.

But can its understanding of Being be, at the preconceptual level, impeccably correct? If it were so, how could we explain the fact that philosophers, when they attempt to conceptualize this understanding, so often get it wrong? If philosophers get things wrong, then at some level everyday Dasein must get them wrong. To suggest otherwise is to make philosophers a breed apart, their theories unrelated to everyday Dasein's (and their own) preconceptual understanding of Being, though with some affinity to the gossip of non-philosophical chatterers. So all of us are fallen, but somehow Heidegger manages to haul himself up.

The jargon of authenticity?

In 1964, Theodor Adorno published *The Jargon of Authenticity*. The complaint embodied in the title is one that Heidegger can appreciate. Jargon is a form of chatter, the reiteration of statements severed from the context of thought, feeling, and perception that originally gave rise to them. Are we then to adopt Heidegger's philosophy as our own, and pass it on to others? Presumably not. That would be chatter and inauthenticity. Are we to follow Heidegger's words only until we have been roused to authenticity and then embark on a philosophical quest of our own? No—that sounds like curiosity, hunger for the new. What we should do is perhaps this: spurred to authenticity by our encounter with Heidegger, we should treat Heidegger as he treated Aristotle, Descartes, or Kant, interpreting and disentangling his work, using it as a basis for new thoughts of our own. (Heidegger describes his approach to other philosophers in various ways: as interpretation, as *Destruktion*—a relative of Derrida's 'deconstruction'—as 'repetition', and, later, as 'conversation'.)

Care

Dasein displays a bewildering variety of characteristics. Heidegger defines its average everydayness as: 'Being-in-the-world which is falling and disclosed, thrown and projecting, and for which its ownmost ability-to-be is an issue, both in its Being alongside the "world" and in its Being-with-others' (BT, 181). No one of these features is basic or 'primordial', such that the rest are derived from it or secondary additions. Being alongside the 'world' (dealing with non-human worldly entities) is not prior to being-with-others (interacting with other people). Nor, conversely, is being-with-others primary and being alongside tools, and so on, a secondary feature derived from it. Again, neither understanding nor mood is primary; both are equally involved in our disclosure of the world and of ourselves. They are equally original or 'equiprimordial'. However, these features are not separable from each other. There could not be an entity that was alongside the 'world' but not with others, or that was with others but not alongside the 'world'. No being could have understanding but no mood, or mood but no understanding. And so on.

How can we bring unity into this account of Dasein? We can do so, if we regard all these features as rooted in Dasein's basic state of care (*Sorge*). *Sorge*, like 'care', has at least two senses: 'caring, worrying' about something, and 'taking care' of things. 'Care', in Heidegger's usage, involves both senses, but its meaning is more fundamental. Even one who is, in the ordinary senses, uncaring, carefree, or careless, is, in Heidegger's sense, caring or careful. It is because Dasein's Being-in-the-world is care that we can speak of its concern (*Besorgen*) about the ready-to-hand, such as shoes and hammers, and its solicitude (*Fürsorge*) for other people. But again concern and solicitude are compatible with neglect, contempt, and hatred; the only entities that lack care, concern, and solicitude are those that are wholly incapable of them, such as stones and trees. (BT conspicuously neglects animals.) Care is distinct from specific attitudes such as willing, wishing, striving, or knowing. To will, wish, or strive for anything one must already care. One must care in order to acquire knowledge. In extreme depression or anxiety, the closest we come to lacking care, we find it hard to will or to wish for anything, even for release from our condition.

Although care embodies Dasein as a whole, it is still complex: 'ahead-of-itself-Being-already-in-(the-world) as Being-alongside (entities encountered within-the-world)' (BT, 192). Care thus involves three constituents. *Dasein is ahead of itself*. It is its possibilities, it is, in a subdued sense, wondering what to do next;

it is up to something. Heidegger associates this with 'existence', with 'understanding', and also with the future. *Dasein is already in the world.* This is associated with 'thrownness' and 'facticity'—the fact that Dasein is 'always already' in a specific situation that determines the possibilities available to it—with the mood that reveals its thrownness, and with the past. *Dasein is alongside entities within the world.* It is engaged in a task, hammering, say, or simply daydreaming. Heidegger associates this with fallenness, and with the present. Care thus embraces and reintegrates what we have so far learned about Dasein, and also implicitly points ahead to Dasein's temporality. Care is correlative to the significance of the world. Only if Dasein is care can it dwell in a significant world, and only if it dwells in a significant world can Dasein be care.

The scandal of philosophy

The first division of BT concludes with the question whether the external world is real or not. Heidegger rejects the question: the 'scandal of philosophy' is not, as Kant supposed, its failure to prove the reality of things outside me, but the fact 'that such proofs are expected and attempted again and again' (BT, 205). There are two connected flaws in the question. It involves an inadequate view of Dasein, of that to which things or the 'world' are supposedly external, and an inadequate view of the Being of things and of the world.

Take Dasein first. Where does the boundary lie between Dasein and what is external to it? Between my body and its environment? Plainly not. It is of no philosophical interest to show that there are things outside my own body; once you have granted that my body exists, you have granted that there is an external world. (Heidegger lived before the days of brains in vats.) Should we locate it between me and the world, then, with my body counted as external to me? Then I am conceived as a pure, 'worldless subject'. This must be a knowing subject, rather than an acting subject, a subject whose only access to the world is by way of internal states of itself—impressions, ideas, or whatever. But this is not what I am like. My Being is care: I potter around doing things in a familiar environment, I am essentially in the world. My access to the world and to things in it is not mediated by ideas or anything of that sort: I hear the 'creaking wagon', not 'pure sounds' (BT, 163), I see trees, not ideas.

Now take things and the world. To view them as 'real' is to view them as present-at-hand. If my Being is care and I am essentially in the world, the world and worldly things cannot be simply present-at-hand. Viewing the world as real is a secondary, derivative way of viewing it, corresponding to the view of Dasein as a bare, worldless subject. The world is a significant field for my careful involvements with it, not a collection of 'external objects'. Things within the world are primarily ready-to-hand—equipment for our use.

A world without Dasein?

But this is not the end of the story. Dasein might not have existed; there might have been no humans at all, as there were once presumably no human beings (BT, 227; cf. xxvi. 216). What would there be in such a 'world'? There would be *beings*, but no *Being*:

> Entities are, quite independently of the experience by which they are disclosed, the acquaintance in which they are discovered, and the grasping in which their nature is ascertained. But Being 'is' only in the understanding of those entities to whose Being something like an understanding of Being belongs.
>
> (BT, 183; cf. xxvi. 194)

Without Dasein there would be no Being. There would be no truth; even Newton's laws would not be true, not disclosed in

Heidegger's sense (BT, 227). There would be no 'world'. But there would be beings or entities, beings without Being. Perhaps Heidegger means that they would have no specific mode of Being. They obviously could not have Dasein's mode of Being. Nor could they be *zuhanden*, like equipment. Might they not be present-at-hand, like rocks and trees? No. Again, this is a way, albeit secondary and derivative, in which Dasein understands things. Even Being of this sort involves disclosure.

Might beings without Being be much as scientists describe them, non-significant collections of particles? But scientists are also Dasein, with all its features and limitations, 'thrown' into a situation they cannot escape. Can we be sure that the discoveries (or 'projections') they make from within this situation accurately portray a world without Dasein? In this spirit R. G. Collingwood quotes J. W. N. Sullivan: 'The second law of thermodynamics is only true because we cannot deal practically with magnitudes below a certain limit. If our universe were populated by intelligent bacteria they would have no need of such a law' (IN, 24 n. 1). Collingwood adds: 'an intelligent organism whose life had a longer time-rhythm than man's might find it not so much unnecessary as untrue' (IN, 26).

Heidegger's response to science is similar, though not exactly similar. He regards science as a secondary phenomenon, only one of Dasein's ways of Being, derivative from and irretrievably dependent on everyday ways of Being. Even scientists use equipment and know their way around the laboratory. But suppose we agree, contrary perhaps to Heidegger's own view, that science gives a fair account of what beings would be like in the absence of Dasein, what would follow from that? We could then say:

1. In the absence of Dasein, things—such as rocks or trees—would be no more than collections of molecules.

Perhaps we would add:

2. Even in the presence of Dasein, things—such as rocks, trees, or hammers—are collections of molecules.

But we might hesitate to say:

3. Things such as hammers are, even in the presence of Dasein, no more than collections of molecules.

Or:

4. Things, such as hammers, are really (in themselves, at bottom) collections of molecules.

Or:

5. Things, such as hammers, are collections of molecules that have significance added to them by Dasein.

Statements 3, 4, and 5 do not obviously follow from statements 1 and 2. Heidegger rejects 5. It goes against the grain of our phenomenal experience to suggest that first we perceive non-significant molecules and then superimpose value. But must ontology mirror phenomenology? Might not a hammer be *only* or *really* a collection of molecules, even if we do not usually view it in that way? It cannot be *only* a collection of molecules, as statement 3 claims. A collection of molecules that is understood or interpreted by Dasein as a hammer is not only a collection of molecules and nothing more. Dasein makes a difference. Something may not be, in a world with Dasein, precisely what it would be in a Dasein-less world. Might it be *really* or in *itself* a collection of molecules and only a hammer superficially or *for us*? But why should we say that? (As Dr Johnson said: 'Pound St Paul's church into atoms, and consider any single atom; it is, to be sure, good for nothing: but, put all these atoms together, and you have St Paul's church.')

The distinction between what is so in itself and what is so only for us is a distinction drawn from our own understanding of Being, not from the Dasein-independent nature of things. If there were no Dasein, there would be no such distinction: every being would be on a par with every other being, with no foreground or background, no depth and no superficiality. We lack resources to describe such a condition: every description we propose is already encumbered with our own understanding of Being, our own significant world. Why should we say that, in our familiar Dasein-ridden world, a hammer is in *itself* a collection of molecules and only *for us* a tool? There is no reason to do so. It follows from no plausible account of a Dasein-free, hammerless world. It gives an unwarranted priority to the theoretical investigations of scientists over the circumspect concern of craftsmen. For such reasons as these Heidegger believes that ontology and phenomenology coincide.

Chapter 7
Time, death, and conscience

Time played only a subdued role in Heidegger's account of average everydayness, though it was implicit in the claim that Dasein is ahead of itself. But time, he said in the Introduction, is crucial to the question of Being: 'the central problematic of all ontology is rooted in the phenomenon of time' (BT, 18). Time is also crucial for the analytic of Dasein: 'Dasein's Being finds its meaning in temporality' (BT, 19).

Why time?

Why Being and Time? Why not Being and Space? Or Truth? Or Nothing? Heidegger does not ask these questions explicitly, but he suggests various answers. Being has traditionally been viewed in terms of time, he argues. The Greek word for 'being', *ousia*, is associated with the word *parousia*, which means *Anwesenheit*, 'presence' (BT, 25). So the Greeks viewed Being in terms of temporal presence. This is incorrect. *Parousia* is only one of several compounds formed from *ousia*; there is no more reason to associate *ousia* with *parousia*-presence than with, say, *apousia*-absence. Moreover, *parousia* can mean spatial presence, one's presence at a battle, say, as well as temporal presence. There may be reason to think that Greeks, at least Greek philosophers, linked Being with temporal presence: Plato ascribed Being only to unchanging, eternal (or eternally *present*) forms or ideas, not to things that 'become', arise, fade, and die away. But Heidegger has not here given such a reason.

He notes also that philosophers often classify entities in terms of time. They distinguish temporal entities such as men, plants, and utterances from atemporal entities such as numbers and propositions, and these again from supratemporal beings such as God (BT, 18). But this can be only an 'indication' that Being is uniquely related to time. Heidegger is ready to resist tradition, when appropriate; he is not entitled to appeal for its support only when it suits him. Moreover, he himself rejects this classification of entities, denying that there are any atemporal or supratemporal entities. There is no supratemporal God in, above, or below Heidegger's world. If there were there might be eternal truths independent of Dasein (cf. BT, 227), but as it is the historic task of uncovering beings falls to finite Dasein, not to God.

Many philosophers in Heidegger's day, especially Husserl, postulated a 'third realm' of sense or meaning—alongside the first realm of physical reality and the second realm of psychological reality. But this, Heidegger remarks, is 'no less questionable than medieval speculation about angels' (xxiv. 306). There are no atemporal propositions, meanings, or theories. These are all ways of Dasein's Being, historical and temporal as Dasein is. The classification to which Heidegger here appeals, then, is one he rejects.

Matters are no better if we look at non-philosophical language. In one of the rare passages in which Heidegger asks 'Why do we not speak just as much of Being and space?' he notes that common vocabulary involves spatial more often than temporal metaphors (xxxi. 119). 'Dasein' itself is a spatial term (xx. 344). This is only natural, since Dasein is as much spatial as it is temporal, and could not exist if it were not.

Why then is time special? One answer is that Dasein lives its life in time in a deeper sense than it lives in space. It is born in a particular place at a particular time, neither of its own choosing. *Where* I am born may be important, if it determines my subsequent acculturation, whether, say, my first language is English or Japanese. But my place of birth is of little *intrinsic* importance. Even if it affects my upbringing I can, if I wish, diminish its effects by travel and study. But *when* I am born has effects that I cannot so readily counteract. If I am born in 1800, I cannot read BT, assuming a maximum human lifespan of about 115 years. The date of my birth limits my position in time, and consequently the courses of action open to me, while the place of my birth does not limit my position in space.

A human being needs space to live in. A life endured in total immobility is, though conceivable, wholly unsatisfactory. But a satisfactory life need not involve extensive travel. One may live well without ever leaving one's native town or village. Conversely, a life requires a decent time-span. Life comprises decisions and activities, and these presuppose, and take, time more crucially than space: I ask what to do now, or next, not what to do here or there.

One difference between authenticity and inauthenticity is that authentic Dasein is not wholly engrossed by the present and by the immediate past and future. Authentic Dasein looks ahead to its death and back to its birth, and beyond its birth to the historical past. Why so? Why not visit faraway places instead, if only in the imagination? One answer is that spatial or geographical travel does not enable one to survey one's life as a whole in the way that temporal or historical awareness does. Another is that my present situation and the possibilities it offers largely depend on the past, both my own past life and the past history of my culture, but hardly at all on what is now happening in remote places. To gain a mastery of my present situation I should read, say, Aristotle—who still influences our present thought—in preference to a contemporary foreign writer who cannot have had such an influence on me. Tradition is handed down over time, not across space. (This is why, when evaluating a work of art or literature, we wonder whether it will 'stand the test of time' rather than the 'test of space'.)

The life of Dasein, then, involves time more vitally than space. There are also two traditional problems about time bearing on Dasein's access to the world. The first exercised Aristotle and St Augustine: only the present moment exists now, the past no longer exists, and the future does not yet exist; so there are no temporally extended objects or events, no world enduring over time, only an instantaneous temporal slice of a world and of the objects and events within it. The second troubled Kant and Husserl as well as ancient thinkers. I can only perceive—see, hear, feel, etc.—what exists at the present moment—or, if we take into account the speed of light and of sound, what existed at some similarly brief past moment. So how can we ever be aware of the past or the future or a temporally enduring world? Neither of these problems concern space. We are not tempted to suppose that what is spatially remote from us does not exist on the ground that it does not exist *here*. Our senses, especially sight, disclose an extensive expanse of space from any given viewpoint.

Heidegger does not tackle these problems explicitly, but was nevertheless troubled by them. His solution, prefigured in part in Aristotle, Augustine, and Kant (BT, 427f.), is this. Dasein's awareness is not confined to the present. It runs ahead into the future and reaches back into the past. Dasein is temporal. Dasein's temporality opens up 'world-time', discloses an enduring world, and makes the world genuinely temporal. Human beings are not just an insignificant biological species that developed on one of many millions of heavenly bodies, a species that has existed for only an insignificant fraction of the history of the universe. Heidegger does not reject the findings of science. Once there was no Dasein, even though there were beings. But such significance as the universe has derives from human beings. It is only this Dasein-derived significance that allows us to say that some things are significant and others trivial. The entry of Dasein into the world was an event of massive import. It was then that history, significance, worldhood, and, in a sense, time itself began. In BT, Dasein takes over some of the functions traditionally assigned to God. Dasein has the advantage that it is finite, in the world, and temporal. Unlike an infinite, supratemporal, unchanging deity, Dasein is open to and opens up a world.

Heidegger does not approach time directly in the second division of BT. He begins with an account of death.

Death

Dasein is always ahead of itself, poised before possibilities as yet unrealized. How then can we get a grip on Dasein as a whole? It seems to elude our grasp, never presenting itself as actual and complete, but always as unfinished business. But there is for Dasein a final possibility, a possibility to end all possibilities, namely death.

This way of introducing death may seem contrived. A person cannot give a complete account of his own life even though he knows that he is going to die, since usually he does not yet know when or how he will die or what will happen in the meantime. However, we may give a more or less complete account of Dasein simply by saying such things as that Dasein is always ahead of itself. We need not specify what possibilities Dasein has or how it will actualize them. It is enough to say that it has possibilities at any moment in its career. We will mention death, since death is an important feature of Dasein. But the possibility of death is not a *uniquely* significant consideration in securing the completeness of the account, just one feature of Dasein among others. 'Oh, by the way,' we might say, 'I mustn't forget to add that this can't go on for ever—Dasein dies one day.'

Heidegger has, however, substantial reasons for bringing in death. Death is not simply something that happens at the end of one's life. Dasein's awareness that it will die, that it may die at any moment, means that 'dying', its attitude to or 'being towards' its own death, pervades and shapes its whole life. A life without the prospect of death would be a life of perpetual postponement. Why bother to write a book now, if I have an eternity of life (and of undiminished physical and mental vigour) before me? Dasein, whether it be a philosopher or an autobiographer, cannot give a complete account of itself without death because death haunts every moment of Dasein's life.

Another reason for introducing death is that death separates, especially sharply, the sheep from the goats, the authentic from the inauthentic. The inauthentic, lost in the anonymity of the 'they', agree that 'one dies'. This is something they chatter about, and chatter ambiguously, referring to suicide, for example, as 'doing something silly'. But they obscure the ever-present possibility, and even the imminence, of my *own* death. They treat dying as a remote possibility, as something that happens to others but not to myself—as long as I do not smoke tobacco, go to war, or 'do something silly'. (They forget to add that whatever reduces my chance of dying of one thing increases my chance of dying of something else.) The authentic person, by contrast, has a constant awareness of the possibility of his own death; he is anxious, though not fearful, in the face of it. He sees his situation and the possibilities it presents to him, and makes a decision among them, in the light of this awareness. Awareness of one's own death snatches one from the clutches of the 'they': since Dasein must die on its own—dying is not a joint or communal enterprise—death 'lays claim to it as an *individual* Dasein … individualizes Dasein down to itself' (BT, 263). This confers on Dasein a peculiar sort of freedom, 'freedom towards death' (BT, 266).

A third reason for introducing death is that it paves the way for Heidegger's account of time. Inauthentic and everyday Dasein are 'ahead of themselves'—they too have possibilities to take up—but they do not anticipate, or 'run ahead into', the possibility of death in the way that authentic Dasein does. But Dasein runs ahead only to its death, not beyond. Death will put an end to its possibilities. This means that 'original' time is *finite*, and ends with my death (BT, 330). *Time* may go on for ever, but *my* time is running out. Does this imply that I cannot reasonably insure my life to provide for my loved ones after my death, or arrange for the posthumous publication of my works? Surely not. It does mean that whatever arrangements I make for post-mortem effects must be made ante-mortem.

The 'future closes one's ability-to-be; that is the future itself is closed' (BT, 330). But the past is not closed in this way; Heidegger shows no inclination to claim that time begins with one's birth as it ends with one's death. For he is vitally interested in history, and history too gives him another reason to consider death. History is made possible by death. Not in this case my own death, but the deaths of our ancestors. History deals with dead Dasein. Past Dasein performed glorious deeds in awareness of its own mortality and it is interestingly different from ourselves because it is dead, but not gone.

Dying

'Taken ontically the results of the analysis [of death] show the peculiar formality and emptiness of any ontological characterization' (BT, 248). To take the results 'ontically' is to take them as factual claims about Dasein's *Ableben*, its death or demise as a living creature. To take them 'ontologically' is to take them as philosophical claims about the Being of Dasein and about its *Sterben*, about Dasein's dying *as* Dasein. Heidegger's results comprise the following propositions:

1. It is certain that I shall die.
2. I have to do my dying for myself. On particular occasions someone else may die in my place, as they may pay my

telephone bill, or attend a meeting, on my behalf. But sooner or later I shall die in person, not by proxy.

3. That I shall die is not merely empirically likely or even empirically certain. If anyone seems not to know about death, this is really because he is 'fleeing in the face of' death (BT, 251).
4. Death will terminate all my possibilities. I cannot do anything after I am dead.
5. It is not certain when I shall die.
6. It is possible that I shall die at any moment.
7. Dying confers wholeness on Dasein.
8. Death is 'non-relational': death severs all one's relationships to others.

Some, but not all, of these propositions look 'formal and empty'. Propositions 1 and 2 are readily acceptable, of interest only insofar as they tend to get covered up. They do not apply uniquely to dying: if I do not die fairly soon, it is certain that I shall sleep and urinate, and that I shall do so in person. Proposition 3 is doubtful. Surely I come to know that I shall die inductively, on the basis of the previous deaths of others of my kind and also my experience of my own ageing. Heidegger agrees that 'demise' may be only 'empirically certain', but adds that this 'is in no way decisive as to the certainty of death' (BT, 257). If so, 'death' must be distinct from bodily 'demise'. If the death of Dasein entailed its bodily demise, then the fact that its bodily demise is only empirically certain would entail that its death is only empirically certain.

Heidegger's point is not that death and bodily demise are quite distinct events—as if a person might die as Dasein, while its body remains alive, or survive as Dasein beyond the death of its body. Death and demise are more or less simultaneous, except possibly in cases such as Nietzsche's, where bodily demise is preceded by a long period of insanity. Heidegger's idea is that my software, Dasein, is primary, and my hardware, the body, conforms to it. Thus I know non-empirically that I shall die as Dasein, but empirically that I shall die as a living organism. It does not follow that either death or demise *could* occur without the other, even if I can *imagine* one of them occurring without the other. But how can I know non-empirically that I shall die?

Proposition 4 is also questionable. I can make arrangements, while alive, for what is to happen after my death. Moreover, belief in a 'life after death' has been, and perhaps still is, quite widespread. Heidegger claims that his 'ontological' account leaves this possibility open:

> If 'death' is defined as the 'end' of Dasein—that is to say, of Being-in-the-world—this does not imply any ontical decision whether 'after death' still another Being is possible, either higher or lower, or whether Dasein 'lives on' or even 'outlasts' itself and is 'immortal'.
>
> (BT, 247f.)

Heidegger's account might be accepted by anyone, whether or not they believe in immortality; this issue can be properly discussed only after we have given such a non-committal account of death. But is his account really compatible with immortality? If Dasein is essentially in the world, how could it survive as Dasein once it is no longer in the world? If it does not survive as Dasein, what else might it survive as? Or might Dasein after death somehow continue to be in a world, retaining a ghostly presence in this world, or passing into another world? Heidegger barely allows a place for beliefs such as these. Yet implausible as they are, they are not so obviously absurd that denial of them is 'formal and empty'.

Proposition 5 is true enough. Even if I resolve to kill myself at a definite time, it is not certain that I shall live until then, that I shall carry out my resolve, or that the bomb will go off on time. Proposition 6 seems to follow from 5, but in fact it does not. It is not possible that I shall die in 200 years' time, though this is because it is certain that I shall die within the next 100 years; it is uncertain when I shall die only within limits. But the main problem with proposition 6 lies not in what it says but in what it does *not* say. Though it is *possible* that I shall die at, or before, 10 o'clock this evening, it is very *unlikely*. My ordering of my life depends on my certainty that I shall die at some time and my uncertainty when I shall die. I would not be writing this book now, if I knew that I would live for ever, or if I knew that I was going to die at 10 o'clock tonight. But equally I would not do so if I did not think it fairly likely that I would live to complete it.

Why does Heidegger neglect probability, when it is as important for the management of my life as possibility? Partly because he associates probability with statistics concerning the longevity of man as a biological species (BT, 246). They deal with demise rather than death. And even if the statistics concern people of my type—elderly English male sedentary pipe-smoking academics—they do not concern my death in particular, but the deaths of people of my *type*. But it is hard to see how a reasonable ordering of one's life could dispense with some estimate of one's life expectancy, whether it be based on informal observation of the fate of relevantly similar others or on how one 'feels in oneself'.

A second reason why Heidegger neglects probability is that Dasein is its possibility, Dasein can decide how to be. Does this mean that at any moment I can kill myself? This seems unlikely. It is not true that one can kill oneself at any moment, even if it is possible for one to die at that moment. He quotes with approval an old saying: 'As soon as a man comes to life, he is at once old enough to die.' True enough. One can die in infancy. But one cannot usually kill oneself in infancy. Nor can one do so if one is asleep, hopelessly drunk, or bound in chains. Again, Heidegger disapproves of suicide as a response to the possibility of death, since it converts the possibility into an actuality instead of letting it remain a possibility (xx. 439). The very inadequacy of this argument suggests that he has a deeply rooted prejudice against suicide and does not have it in mind when he speaks of the constant possibility of death. If death is a possibility, but not a possibility that is, in the usual sense, to be chosen, why can we not speak of death at a given moment or within a given period as probable or as unlikely?

Proposition 7 supplies Heidegger's best argument for the view that Dasein knows non-empirically that it will die. Dasein is care; it orders its life by undertaking various projects and allowing a certain time for them. How could it do that if it had an eternity of time at its disposal? It could not, any more than I could be a prudent financial manager if I had an infinite amount of wealth at my disposal. But a prudent manager of life or finances needs to know more than Heidegger allows. He needs to know not just that his life will end or his resources are limited. He needs to know roughly how long he can expect to live, or how much wealth he has. I cannot manage my funds wisely if I do not know whether I have £10 billion or £100. I cannot manage my life prudently if I have no idea whether I shall live for one minute or 500 years. If in the natural course of events people matured at around 20 years of age and then had 500 years of active life ahead of them, they might be more averse to risk, less ready to sacrifice their remaining centuries in wars or on mountain peaks than we are to forgo the years or decades left to us.

Heidegger does not allow Dasein enough knowledge to exist as care. But what it requires to exist as care need not be *knowledge*. If I believe that I have about £100,000 available, I may manage my funds prudently—even if in fact and unbeknown to myself I have £10 billion or even an infinity of wealth. Likewise, Dasein may exist as care if it *thinks* it will die at around 75, even if it will in fact live far longer or even forever. Unlike the prudent fund manager, Dasein is bound to realize sooner or later that it has far more years available than it originally supposed (unless it is subject to periodic memory loss), though it need never establish that it is immortal. What matters for care is not so much that

Dasein *will* die, but that it *believes* that it will die. Heidegger need not disagree with this: the important thing for him is 'dying', one's being towards death, not dying or death in the ordinary senses.

United in death?

Proposition 8 is connected with propositions 2 and 4. If death puts an end to all my possibilities (4), then I cannot, after my death, be actively related to other people (8); I may be loved or remembered by others, but I cannot love or remember them in return. If I have to die in person, not just by proxy (2), then again I cannot be related, in my death or my dying, to other people by the relation of proxyship or representation. But there is more to proposition 8 than that. Dying is not like loving, where someone is the object of the love even if the love is unrequited. It is not like playing chess, which (usually) requires two people to play together. It is more like solitaire. Even when two or more people die together, they are like people playing solitaire in the same room. Or like two people sleeping together (literally) in the same bed. Everyone, we might say, dies alone. And we can add: everyone sleeps alone.

Usually dying is a solitary business. But must it be so? Why cannot dying, the process of dying, be more like chess or dancing, where what each person does depends on what the other does? We arrange to shoot each other at the same time. Two lovers die of grief, since each believes the other to be dying. Warriors stay to die holding the pass, but each does so only on condition that the others do. Much as lovers fall asleep in each other's arms, each doing so when and because the other does so.

The process of dying, however, terminates in death, the state of being dead. In death one cannot be related to others as one may be in dying. Death is not unique in this respect. In dreamless sleep one cannot be related to others as one may be in falling asleep.

Only we usually wake up from sleep and renew our relations to others. But why, even so, need death 'individualize Dasein down to itself'? There are two reasons for doubting that it must.

Firstly, though one is not, in death, related to others, nor is one a lone individual, immured in solitary confinement. In death, one is not related to others, but not isolated from them either; one simply *is not*. Secondly, although a dead person cannot *from his own point of view* be related to others—since he no longer has a point of view—it may seem to him before his death, and to others after his death, that he has important relations to others in *death*. The Athenians who fell at Marathon, and the Spartans who fell at Thermopylae, were buried together in common graves; it seemed important to their contemporaries that this should be so, to mark their comradeship in death as well as in dying.

Nowadays appropriate burial is supposed to require an individual grave, but people often wish to be buried near to definite others. Heidegger himself wanted to lie beside his parents in Messkirch. When he expressed this wish, the prospect of his death did not individualize him down to his bare self; he was the son of Friedrich and Johanna Heidegger, a native of Messkirch, united in death to his fellow townsmen. Was that inauthentic? No more so, surely, than his concern for the posthumous publication of his works.

But at least, Heidegger might reply, taking seriously the prospect of your own death forces you to consider what relations to which others importantly matter to *yourself*. You can no longer remain dispersed in the inauthenticity of the *they*, content to be buried with your family (or with your fallen comrades) simply because that is what 'one' does. Can I not? Is it less reasonable to submit to custom in the disposal of my corpse than in the choice of my clothes? Still, Heidegger believed, at this stage of his career at least, that dying individualizes Dasein: 'In a way, it is only in dying that I can say absolutely "I am"' (xx. 440).

Authentic Dasein runs ahead to its own death. How does it do that? The answer lies in conscience.

Conscience

If Dasein runs ahead to its own death, it can escape the clutches of the 'they' and make an authentic choice about its own way of Being, not simply accept the limited range of possibilities allowed by 'them'. But how can it do that? 'They' already cater for death. *They* tell me not to worry about it, it's a remote possibility. So Dasein remains in the embrace of the 'they'. In this condition Dasein does not really have a conscience, it is not responsible for what it is and does, and it is not guilty of anything. 'They' take responsibility for things, since all I am and do I am and do because it is what 'one' is and does. Guilt and responsibility are placed on 'their' shoulders. I do not even make real choices: I just follow the routines that 'they' prescribe.

Conscience in the traditional sense commands or forbids actions on moral grounds. Often it is regarded as a voice that calls to one, sometimes as the voice of God. In this sense of 'conscience', someone mired in the they-self lacks a conscience. Conscience tells *me* what to do and what not to do, me as an individual self, not the they-self. It may tell me not to do what *they* do, or to do what they do not do. If I have not yet eluded the they-self, I cannot have a conscience in this sense: I do not view myself as an individual distinct from others, making choices on my own account.

Heidegger uses the same word, *Gewissen*, both for conscience in this traditional sense and for conscience in his more fundamental sense, but it is convenient to distinguish them as, respectively, 'conscience' and 'Conscience'. Not everyone has a conscience, but everyone has a Conscience. A Conscience tells me not what specific choices to make or avoid, but calls on me to make a choice, to take action, and to bear my own responsibility for it. Before

I can choose, I have to choose to choose, and it is to this choice that Conscience calls me. Only when I have chosen choice, answered the call of Conscience, can I have a conscience. If I hear the call of Conscience, it is because I want to have a conscience. Everyone has a Conscience and it calls to them continuously. Not everyone responds to it, and no one responds all the time. That is why the call of conscience is only intermittent.

If I am wholly in thrall to the 'they', how can I ever hear the call of Conscience? How can there be a call of Conscience? The call does not come from God, nor from any third party. This would not help to answer our question. We could still ask: why do some hear God's call and others not? Does he call louder to some and more softly to others? Or are some heavier sleepers than others? Then the call of Conscience would be like an alarm clock ringing just loud enough to wake light sleepers. But the call does not come from outside. It comes from Dasein itself; Dasein calls to Dasein. It comes from Dasein itself, because Dasein is never wholly and irretrievably lost in the *they*. Dasein retreats into the security of the *they* owing to a 'fleeing of Dasein in the face of itself—of itself as an authentic ability-to-be-its-Self' (BT, 184). But Dasein must have a glimpse of that from which it flees. It is this residual awareness of its authentic self that enables Dasein both to call to itself and on occasion respond to the call.

Guilt and nullity

When Dasein responds to the call of Conscience, does it want to have a conscience as well as a Conscience? Does it acquire a conscience in the traditional sense? Heidegger does not seem to answer these questions in the affirmative. The call of Conscience, like that of conscience, reveals to Dasein that it is *guilty*. But Guilt in this sense (again the capital 'G' marks Heidegger's special usage) is not something to which Dasein succumbs only occasionally. Every Dasein is Guilty, but only authentic Dasein realizes its Guilt and acts in full awareness of it. The idea of a primordial, ineradicable Guilt is not original to Heidegger. He ascribes it to Goethe: 'The agent is, as Goethe also said, always unscrupulous [*gewissenlos*, 'conscienceless']. I can only be really unscrupulous, when I have chosen wanting-to-have-a-conscience' (xx. 441). It is only because everyone is Guilty that anyone can be guilty.

Why is Dasein Guilty? Several ideas are in play. Dasein makes a choice *itself*; it cannot unload the responsibility onto *them* or someone else. Dasein chooses one possibility from among several; it inevitably neglects some worthwhile possibilities in favour of its chosen course. Any choice has unforeseen and unintended consequences, but for these too it must take responsibility. An authentic choice may well break the rules established by *them*. Above all, when Dasein makes its choice, choosing its way of Being not for the next two days but for its whole life, it has no ultimate reason for making this choice rather than an alternative: 'we define the formal existential idea of the "Guilty" as: Being-the-basis for a Being which has been defined by a "not" that is, as Being-the-basis of a nullity' (BT, 283).

Why is Dasein the basis of a nullity? In average everydayness, Dasein's decisions follow naturally from what it has done earlier. I have promised, say, to have Martin's shoes ready by tomorrow, so I should start work on them this afternoon. Even if I face a dilemma—should I allow Martin credit, and if so, how much?—there are well-established procedures for resolving it. *They* know what I should do in such situations; I can always do what they say I should.

But it is different if I am choosing the course of my whole life. Shall I remain a shoemaker or shall I become a missionary or enter politics? Nothing in my past life naturally favours one of these options, since I am deciding not what step to take next within a predetermined life-plan, but how my life should go as a whole. It is no use consulting *them*. They will likely say it would be silly to give up making shoes. But what they say is no longer relevant. I am choosing my own life, not theirs, and the fact that I am doing so implies that I have broken free of their grip. Running ahead to my death and turning back to my birth has replaced appeal to the they-self as a way of deciding matters. But then my choice lacks any basis outside itself. The life I project for myself is a nullity. Matters look no better if I reflect on my range of options. This is no longer a menu presented to me by *them*, but it is restricted by a situation that I did not myself choose. I cannot become a knight in armour or an astronaut. In contrast to the everyday view of things, the life-choice to which Conscience calls me seems thoroughly contingent. As Dr Johnson said: 'To prefer one future mode of life to another, upon just reasons, requires faculties which it has not pleased our Creator to give us.'

Resoluteness

What then does authentic Dasein do? It becomes resolute, *entschlossen*, a word related to *erschlossen*, 'disclosed', and itself meaning literally 'dis-, un-closed': 'Resoluteness [*Entschlossenheit*] is a distinctive mode of Dasein's disclosedness [*Erschlossenheit*]' (BT, 297). Resoluteness discloses Dasein itself in a new way; Dasein surveys its life as a whole from its birth to its death. It discloses the world and worldly things, including other people, in a new way. It thus discloses a range of possibilities that are not visible to everyday Dasein, lost in the they.

Heidegger's account of resoluteness is coloured by his study of the conversions of St Paul, St Augustine, and Martin Luther. Paul is in the same world after seeing the light on the road to Damascus as he was before, but everything looks different. Resoluteness confers on Dasein's decisions a fateful necessity despite the nullity of its projection: Luther says not 'Perhaps this is what I should do', but 'Here I stand; I cannot do otherwise.' In resoluteness Dasein pulls itself together as well as opens itself up. Later in BT Heidegger uses the term *Augenblick*—literally 'eye-glance', but the ordinary German for 'instant' or 'moment'—for the 'moment of vision' in which resolute Dasein assesses the possibilities implicit in its situation and makes a decisive choice.

What choice should resolute Dasein make? Can its choice be right or wrong? Are there any criteria for telling whether it is right or wrong? Conscience in the traditional sense is often held to be open to error. Can resoluteness err? Heidegger gives no indication that it can, or that there is any way in which a choice might be assessed apart from the resoluteness in which it is made. Authentic Dasein cannot simply follow what they say about right and wrong, nor can it appeal to any established moral code. Any code or criterion suggested to it is itself something that has to be chosen or rejected.

Karl Löwith records a joke devised by one of Heidegger's students: 'I am resolved, only towards what I don't know' (Löwith, 30). This is unfair. A resolute person knows very well what he must do, even if it is only that he, like Paul, must wait for God's command. But there is no single thing that every resolute person has to do, nor are there any rules by which we, or a given person, can decide what to do. Heidegger himself was resolute in the pursuit of philosophy, but this is not something he could recommend to everyone or even to those equipped for it.

Heidegger always declined to write a work on ethics: a 'concrete moral code' does not depend on our possession of an 'ethic as an absolutely binding science' (xvii. 85). We all know, without the help of philosophy or ethics, that we should, in normal circumstances, pay our debts and keep our promises. But when it comes to momentous choices about the conduct of our lives, a concrete moral code is of little help. Either it gives no unequivocal answer to our problem or it is itself open to question. But an 'ethic as an absolutely binding science' would be no use either. It too leaves the matter undecided or is open to question.

Heidegger's attitude to fundamental choices is similar to his view of truth. There is no truth in the sense of correspondence to the facts, nor are there, in the most fundamental cases, any criteria for telling whether a view is true or not. The best one can do is to be 'primordial', to go back as far as one can towards the source, disregarding the current wisdom of the they. So it is with choice. There are no objectively correct answers to life's basic problems nor any decision procedure for resolving them. The best one can do is to be resolute, to withdraw from the crowd, and to make one's decision in view of one's life as a whole. One's choices, like one's assertions, are always made in a specific situation. What looks good to me in this situation may not look so good to others now or later, or even to myself in a later situation. There is no remedy for that. The only guarantee that what I do now will meet with my approval twenty years hence is to postpone it for twenty years.

Why be resolute?

One Dasein heeds the call of Conscience and in resolute authenticity runs ahead to its death. Another Dasein does not. Is the former better than the latter? If so, why? Why is it better to be resolute than to drift with the tide of everydayness? If Heidegger were recommending resoluteness, he would be proposing a sort of ethic. Not, it is true, a very definite ethic as far as our conduct is concerned. Resolute Dasein need not decide to abandon shoemaking in favour of some more exhilarating mode of life. But if it does continue making shoes, it does so 'with the sober anxiety which brings us face to face with our individualized ability to be,...an unshakable joy in this possibility' (BT, 310). This, he implies, is better than making shoes simply because it never occurs to you to do anything else.

Resoluteness is not *morally* better than irresoluteness. It does not guarantee morally better conduct or even make it more likely. (Hitler was no less resolute than Christ or Socrates.) Nor is resoluteness intrinsically morally superior to irresoluteness. The advantage of resoluteness is that resolute Dasein discloses itself, its possibilities, and its wholeness, in a way that irresolute Dasein does not. Everyday fallen Dasein tends to misinterpret itself: 'the entity which we ourselves are, is ontologically that which is farthest' (BT, 311; cf. BT, 15). (Cf. lxiii. 32: 'Dasein speaks of itself, it sees itself in a certain way, and yet it is only a mask, which it holds before itself so that it does not terrify itself.')

We need to look at resolute Dasein to see what Dasein is really like, but this begs several questions. Does Heidegger suppose that resolute Dasein is *really* Dasein in a way that irresolute Dasein is not? If so, with what right? Most of us for most of the time are irresolute. Why assume that we come into our own only when we are resolute? Or that only resolute Dasein sees itself as it really is? If irresolute Dasein interprets itself as a thing among other things or as one of the crowd, why assume that it is wrong to do so? Resolute Dasein may not be a *thing*, but perhaps irresolute Dasein is.

Heidegger's reply is this. Both resoluteness and irresoluteness, both authenticity and inauthenticity, are ways of Dasein's being. In this respect neither has priority over the other. But irresolute, inauthentic Dasein cannot give an adequate interpretation of its own condition or of resoluteness. Similarly, when one is asleep or daydreaming one cannot give an adequate account *either* of sleep and daydreaming *or* of wakefulness and alertness. To interpret everydayness or dispersal in the 'they' requires a withdrawal from, or elevation above, these states. Heidegger was influenced by Plato's allegory in the *Republic*: ordinary men are prisoners in a cave, looking at shadows on the wall; some escape into the world above, where they see real objects and eventually the sun itself; they return into the cave to persuade the other prisoners to escape. Only an escapee can give a proper account of the condition in the cave, as well as of what is outside the cave.

Similarly, only the resolute can give an account of irresolution or of resoluteness. To be a philosopher one must be resolute. One must, first, withdraw from the round of everydayness, then rise above the current philosophical situation and the tradition that lies behind it. One cannot, if one wants to do more than humdrum routine philosophy, simply absorb the concepts, doctrines, and problems handed down by tradition. One has to run ahead to one's own death and return to the past, back to the source of the philosophical tradition. Then one masters the tradition and is not mastered by it. One has left *them* far behind. As Heidegger puts it: 'the research which wants to develop and conceptualize that kind of Being which belongs to existence, is itself a kind of Being which disclosive Dasein possesses; can such research be denied this projecting which is essential to Dasein?' (BT, 315). No more, surely, than Dasein can be expected to philosophize in its sleep.

Chapter 8
Temporality, transcendence, and freedom

Time has now come into its own. Dasein can only be resolute in time or over time. But we should not say that Dasein is 'in' time or 'over' time. Time is not a container that Dasein is in, any more than the world is. In fact what is primary is not time (*Zeit*), but Dasein's timeliness or temporality (*Zeitlichkeit*). This is a standard move in Heidegger: the primary phenomenon is not the world, space, time, or history, but Dasein's Being-in-the-world, Dasein's spatiality, Dasein's temporality, or Dasein's historicity. What looks like a thing or substance, denoted by a concrete noun, becomes a way of Dasein's being, denoted by an adjective or abstract noun. Dasein is placed at the centre of things: 'Time is Dasein' (CT, 20).

Moreover, time is my time, the time of an individual Dasein: 'Insofar as time is in each case mine, there are many times. Time itself is meaningless; time is temporal' (CT, 21). It sounds as if time is hopelessly subjective (if it were not for Heidegger's insistence that Dasein is not a 'subject')—as if each resolute agent had its own time, ending with its own death and unrelated to the time of any other agent. But matters are not left there. Intersubjective 'world-time', *the* time that is the same for all Dasein, is restored—as a derivative phenomenon, but nonetheless real.

There are in BT at least four notions of time or temporality: 'primordial' or 'authentic' temporality, the temporality of resolute

Dasein; inauthentic temporality, the temporality of everyday fallen Dasein; world-time, the public time in which we encounter beings within the world; and finally 'vulgar' or 'ordinary' time, time as conceived by philosophers from Aristotle to Bergson, time as a homogeneous, unending sequence of 'nows' or instants.

Each of these notions (except the first) derives from the preceding. This too is a regular feature of Heidegger's procedure. He does not begin (as Husserl might do) from the apparently simpler phenomenon—time as a sequence of instants, or, in other cases, living organisms or the merely present-at-hand—and then construct from this the more complex phenomenon: authentic temporality, Dasein, or the ready-to-hand. He begins with the richer, more complex phenomenon and derives the simpler phenomenon from it by successively 'modifying' it. Non-human animals, for example, are to be understood 'privatively', as creatures that lack certain features of Dasein; Dasein is not to be seen as an animal with something else, reason say, added to it.

Heidegger proceeds in this way, from the complex to the simple, for reasons both of phenomenology and of ontology. We do not naturally view ourselves as animal organisms with reason superimposed on them, or the time of our decision as a sequence of homogeneous instants with significance conferred upon it by our resolution. The complex is not *composite*: it is not constructed by the combination of simpler elements, and it cannot be analysed as if it were. Our experience of time did not first enter the world as a tedious now-sequence; it first arose as the time of resolute Dasein, Dasein striving to impose order and significance on an apparently hostile or indifferent environment.

Authentic temporality

Resolute Dasein runs ahead to its death, and reaches back into the past, before deciding what to do in the present, the authentic present or *Augenblick*, the moment of vision. It returns to the past, since it cannot fully grasp its present situation or decide how to act unless it knows how it reached its present situation. I cannot decide how to continue writing unless I know something about what I have written earlier. This is so, even if the continuation is relatively unproblematic. I shall need to explore my earlier writing, and perhaps beyond, more seriously if my decision is more problematic, if, say, I have decided to restructure the book entirely or I have got into a muddle owing to some false assumption I have accepted all along.

Resolute Dasein goes back even further. How far and where to? Back to Messkirch in 1889? Or back to Plato in the 4th century BCE? Heidegger occasionally mentions birth: 'Dasein exists as born; and, as born, it is already dying, in the sense of Being-towards-death. As long as Dasein factically exists, both the "ends" and their "between" *are*' (BT, 374). But he does not mention birth nearly as often as death; nor does he suggest that time begins with one's birth as it ends with one's death. This is reasonable. One's active life begins with one's birth as it ends with one's death. But the past time that bears on one's present situation need not begin with one's birth. In some decisions one reverts to one's birth. In deciding to be buried in Messkirch Heidegger needed to recall that he was born there. Other decisions invoke a larger span of the past. In deciding to reconsider the question of being he needed to return to ancient philosophers, not simply to the philosophy written after his birth. Anything one does can be considered *both* in the context of one's own life *and* in the larger context of a historical tradition.

Heidegger's marriage and his burial belong to a tradition of marriages and of burials as well as to his own life. BT too is an event in Heidegger's life as well as a stage in the philosophical tradition that began in the 7th century BCE. It seems appropriate, when deciding on marriage or burial, to focus on one's own life and simply take the tradition for granted. But it would not be natural to do this when deciding how to write a work such as BT.

One's own life is relevant to the decision *whether* to write a book at all. But once one has decided to write a philosophy book, one's own life (including, say, one's prospects of gaining tenure) recedes into the background, and the philosophical tradition comes into sharper focus. Conversely, in running ahead into the future, I cannot go far beyond my own death. Quite likely philosophy, as well as other things, will continue after my death, but my idea of what it will be like is too hazy for me to take much account of it. At most I can arrange for the posthumous publication of my works, though their fate is uncertain and beyond my control.

Resolute Dasein has a future ending with its death, a past extending back to its birth and perhaps beyond, and a present. Heidegger calls these 'ecstases', from a Greek word meaning 'standing outside, forth', hence 'removal, displacement', and, later, 'being beside oneself, or out of one's mind, in an ecstatic mental state'. ('Ecstasis' is related to 'existence' and has the same root meaning.) Temporality essentially involves these ecstases. They do not figure, except as later additions, in the conception of time as a series of instants. What matters to Galileo as a physicist is *how long* two balls of different weights take to roll down a slope, not whether they do so in the past, present, or future. But Galileo decided to perform this experiment, and this decision involved the ecstatic temporality of resolute Dasein, with a past, present, and future.

The future is the primary ecstasis, certainly for resolute Dasein, but also, with 'modification', for irresolute Dasein. Time is essentially and primarily time for doing something, time to do something, and this involves the future more immediately than the past or present. The German for 'future' is *Zukunft*, literally 'to-coming, coming to(wards)'; the root idea is that events come to us out of the future. Heidegger interprets it differently: Dasein runs ahead to its own death and then 'comes towards itself' out of the future. It does not return simply to the present. It recoils from the future, from its own death, back into the past.

The ordinary German for the 'past' is *Vergangenheit*. But this suggests to Heidegger the past as dead and gone. The past to which Dasein rebounds is the past that lives on in the present, the past that informs its present situation and its inherent possibilities. For this he uses *Gewesenheit*, 'having-been-ness'. Dasein's past is not something dead and gone that it has left behind. The relevant past, the past that bears on its present situation, emerges from the future. Dasein then rebounds from the past into the present and there it decides on action.

The ordinary German for the 'present' is *Gegenwart*, literally 'waiting towards', but Heidegger gives it an active flavour by associating it with a verb, *gegenwärtigen*, to 'make present': 'Only as the Present in the sense of making present, can resoluteness be what it is: namely, letting itself be encountered undisguisedly by that which it seizes upon in taking action' (BT, 326). 'Making present' is to the present what 'retaining' is to the past and 'waiting' or expecting is to the future; Heidegger avoids anything so specific and detached as 'perceiving'. Irresolute, as well as resolute, Dasein has a *Gegenwart*. Only resolute Dasein has an *Augenblick*, a moment of vision.

Temporality and care

Dasein's ability at any moment to traverse its whole life—to run ahead to its death, return to its birth, and rebound into the present—is what makes it a unified self: Dasein bursts asunder into past, present, and future and then pulls itself together again—more like a piece of elastic than beads on a string.

The triadic structure of temporality corresponds to other triads in Heidegger's account of Dasein. Heidegger 'repeats' or reworks his earlier results in view of their temporality. Care has a threefold structure: it is '[1] ahead-of-itself-[2] Being-already-in-(the-world) as [3] Being-alongside (entities encountered within-the-world)' (BT, 192).

Being ahead of oneself involves primarily the future. Every Dasein is ahead of itself, is up to something. In resoluteness this takes the form of running ahead to death, while in inauthenticity it is diluted to 'awaiting', waiting to see what will happen and being ready to deal with it. Understanding, too, is essentially directed to the future: it is knowing how to cope with things and, in its most authentic form, knowing how to live. With the future too belongs existence, Dasein's supervision of its own being.

The second element of care, being already in the world, involves the past. Dasein has been 'thrown' into the world, it is encumbered with 'facticity', contingent features of itself and of its situation that are not its doing and that it simply has to make the most of. Thrownness and facticity are disclosed by moods such as anxiety, which are primarily directed to the past. (Anxiety is past-directed, since it is 'anxious about naked Dasein as something that has been thrown into uncanniness' (BT, 343). Anxiety's inauthentic counterpart, fear, is also past-directed, since it involves having 'forgotten oneself' in one's bewilderment (BT, 342).)

The third element, being alongside entities encountered within the world, primarily involves the present, 'making present', in the sense of 'letting oneself be encountered by', things in one's current situation. Falling too pertains to the present: fallen Dasein concerns itself with what is present, its immediate business or the current gossip, rather than the long-term past or future. Talk or discourse, which ranks alongside understanding, mood, and falling as a central feature of Dasein, does not belong to any ecstasis, but ranges over all three; tenses are essential to discourse.

Temporality and Being-in-the-world

Everyday Dasein is mostly irresolute. It need not be fickle and vacillating; it has its job to do and concentrates on that, without bothering whether this is a fitting way to spend its life. It is absorbed in the present rather than the future. It wields a tool, a hammer say, to bang a nail into leather. But 'one tool is ontologically impossible' (BT, 353). A tool always belongs to an implicit network of interreferential equipment in the workplace. (The 'impossibility' is only 'ontological': Heidegger does not exclude the 'ontical' possibility of my having only one tool because the others have been stolen or lost in a shipwreck. He does exclude the possibility that I have invented a wheel but have not yet thought of anything to do with it.)

When I use the hammer, I make it present. It is what I am focusing on at present. How then is the workshop as a whole *there* for me? It could not be, if I did no more than make things present. I do not at present have the whole workshop in my sights, nor do I see or explicitly think about my customers. I 'retain' the equipment that I am not presently using, my customers, and so on. I have a muted awareness of their presence. I have somehow forgotten them too, just as I have forgotten myself in my absorption in my task. This is the everyday relationship to the past.

Similarly I 'await' or expect certain things—in a subdued sense quite distinct from that in which I expect my horse to win. I expect my hammer to function properly, I expect my nails to be there when I want another, I do not expect to touch a rat as I reach for a nail. I notice broken tools, missing tools, and unexpected intruders. I could not do this, if 'concernful dealings were merely a sequence of "experiences" running their course "in time"'. All this must 'be grounded in the ecstatical unity of the making-present which awaits and retains' (BT, 355). So it is time that makes possible Being-in-the-world, time as ecstatic temporality.

Time, transcendence, and freedom

Occasionally in BT (364ff.), but more often in later works (xxvi; ER), Heidegger identifies Being-in-the-world with Dasein's 'transcendence'. This does not mean that Dasein is or attains to some otherworldly entity, nor that it manages to surmount the barriers of its own subjectivity and make contact with an external object—there are no such barriers. Dasein transcends, steps beyond, every particular entity to the world in which they lie. What if Dasein did not transcend? Stones do not transcend, nor do insects, dogs, or God. Stones, insects, and dogs are in varying degrees crowded in by the things in their environment. Everything they do is determined by their immediate surroundings. Things are too close, too oppressive, to be 'encountered'. God too cannot encounter entities, not because they crowd him in, but because they are wholly his creation, wholly and eternally transparent to him and at his beck and call. Conversely, Dasein transcends other entities and projects a world in which they lie at a critical distance from Dasein itself. Thus Dasein is (unlike God) finite, in the midst of beings which it allows to be themselves, and thus encounters rather than creates. But (unlike stones or animals) Dasein has free space in which to live, beyond the control of its immediate environment or of any given entity. Dasein leaves things alone and they leave it alone.

Take an analogy: in a self-enclosed hierarchical group (a patriarchal family, say) the members cannot choose their relationships—to whom and how they relate. Those at the bottom are at the bidding of those above; their every relationship and much of their conduct is moulded by their superiors. These are the insects. The person at the top of the hierarchy has all those below in his control; what they do is determined by him. He is God. Neither the insects nor God encounter genuine *others*, only immovable oppressors or pliant vassals. But Dasein transcends every such other and every such relationship. It need not associate with this person or that, in this way or that. It can choose its 'being-with', how and with whom it associates. It can let the others be as they are, independent others who are not at its beck and call as it is not at theirs. Not that Dasein can do as it likes. Others place constraints on it. Dasein is not God. So it is with Dasein's Being-in-the-world. Dasein allows free play to other beings, including other Dasein, and they leave it free space. Only then can it encounter other beings. It does not first encounter other beings, and then superimpose worldhood and significance on them. It cannot encounter them at all unless it transcends them to a world and then returns from it to particular entities, as a spider spins a web and encounters flies within it. Dasein steers a path too between realism and idealism. If realism, or materialism, were right it would be like an insect. If idealism were right, it would be like God. But Dasein is in-between: between God and insects, between birth and death, and between itself and the world.

Dasein's transcendence depends on ecstatic temporality of a sort that no other entity has, Dasein has a future, a past, and a present. Each ecstasis is a 'horizon' or rather a field bounded by a horizon. Each is defined by one of three aspects of purposive activity, and this is its 'horizonal schema' or 'pattern'. Firstly, the 'for the sake of itself', Dasein's aims and purposes—the schema of the future. (Dasein is not essentially *egotistical*. My aim may be to help others, but it is nevertheless *my* aim.) Secondly, that 'in the face of which' Dasein is thrown, the background situation not of my own making—the schema of the past. Finally, the 'in order to', the equipment I use to achieve my purposes and aims—the schema of the present.

Ecstatic temporality transcends particular entities in two respects. Firstly, an ecstasis is not simply the aggregate of things and events encountered in it. I run ahead into the future knowing little about what will happen in the future, apart from my own chronologically indeterminate death. When I return to the past, I do not retrace every past event in reverse chronological order until I reach, say, my birth. I have forgotten most of these events, even those I once experienced, so I return without more ado to the relevantly significant past.

Secondly, ecstatic temporality treats particular entities as possibilities rather than actualities. The past into which I am thrown is significant not for what it starkly is, but for the possibilities it presents for continuing my life. The hammer on the bench is not just something actual. It is something I may or may not use, something I may use for this purpose or for that, beyond the hammer itself and my use of it. Dasein transcends its own present state. The interest of my present state lies in what it enables me to do or become.

So Dasein transcends to world and transcends in temporality. These ways of transcending look similar in structure. But why should we agree that they are essentially connected—that Dasein transcends temporally if, and only if, it transcends to world, let alone that worldly transcendence is based on temporal transcendence? No doubt there could be no world, in Heidegger's sense, without temporality. But might there not be temporality without a world? There could not, for two reasons.

Firstly, there cannot be temporality without entities besides Dasein itself. Time is not just a series of nows. It is time for doing things with things. Time is dated by reference to things and events, the time of my birth, say, or the time of so-and-so's death. Moreover, things and events cannot simply be strung out along time without belonging, even at a single time, to a world. The nails I shall need later are even now in the cupboard. Messkirch, where I was once born and where one day I shall be buried, is there even now, though I have not been there for some time. Time spills over into the world. Secondly, Dasein's freedom, which is secured by its temporality, requires Being-in-a-world. Given that there are beings, Dasein must transcend them, place them in a world, and keep them at a distance.

Is Dasein really free? Are its choices and actions not caused by, or grounded in, other things and events out of its control? Not on Heidegger's view. In later works he argues that grounds presuppose Dasein's freedom rather than eradicate it (xxvi; xxxi; ER). If entities were regarded as simply actual, we would not ask after their grounds. We only ask for the ground or cause of something, the French Revolution, say, or Stonehenge, if we regard it as possibly otherwise, as only one possibility among others.

But it is Dasein's freedom and transcendence that enables, indeed requires, it to view entities as possibilities rather than sheer actualities. Hence Dasein asks for the grounds of things. It asks 'why?': 'Man is not primarily the no-sayer..., nor is he the yes-sayer; he is the why-asker' (xxvi. 280). Dasein regards any particular being as a possibility and asks for its ground. It can also ask for the ground of all beings together. It can ask: 'Why is there anything at all rather than nothing?' (xxvi; IM). It asks this, because in its resolute, anxious moments, it views beings as a whole as a possibility rather than a sheer actuality. Thus not only empirical science, but metaphysics—philosophy in the grand manner of Leibniz and Schelling—is rooted in Dasein's freedom: 'metaphysics belongs to the nature of man...to exist is already to philosophize' (xxvi. 274).

Heidegger takes seriously Kant's doctrine of the primacy of practical reason—more seriously, perhaps, than Kant did.

Chapter 9
History and world-time

Heidegger interrupts his account of time in BT to consider, in chapter 5 of Division II, 'Temporality and Historicality'. His interest in history dates back to 1916, when in 'The Concept of Time in the Study of History' he argued that the historian cannot regard time, as the natural scientist does, as purely quantitative and uniform.

Historical time involves qualitatively distinct periods, such as the Victorian era, whose significance depends on more than their number of years. History was a thriving discipline in 19th-century Germany, and philosophy of history followed in its train. Heidegger was impressed by Wilhelm Dilthey (1833–1911), whose collected works began to appear in 1913. As well as being a historian of culture, Dilthey tried to do for history what Kant had done for the natural sciences: to unearth the basic a priori conditions that enable us to study history.

Another significant figure, often mentioned in Heidegger's early lectures though not in BT itself, is Oswald Spengler (1880–1936). In *The Decline of the West* (2 vols, 1918, 1922), Spengler presented the past as a series of distinct, self-contained cultures, each of which undergoes, like a living organism, a process of growth, maturity, and decay. Thought and values are, he believed, relative to a specific culture and have no universal validity.

Even mathematics is culturally determined: ancient Greek mathematics is significantly different from modern mathematics, not simply a fragment of it.

Historical relativism concerned Heidegger as well as other philosophers of the time. In early lectures he quotes Eduard Spranger:

> All of us—Rickert, the phenomenologists, the tendency that starts with Dilthey—we all come together in the great struggle over the timeless in the historical, over the realm of sense and its expression in a concrete culture that has arisen, over a theory of values which leads beyond the merely subjective to objective validity.
>
> (xxi. 91; lxiii. 42)

Heidegger dislikes Spranger's talk about 'values' and the 'realm of sense', dubbing it 'platonism for barbarians' (xxi. 91). But he agrees that relativism is a problem, and argues that there have so far been three solutions. One is Spengler's, giving free rein to the historical and accepting that there is no suprahistorical objectivity, nothing that is as true in 1927 as it was in 500 BCE. Another is Platonism, extracting eternal truths and values from varying historical contexts, if not ignoring history altogether. Spranger favours this solution. So do Descartes and Husserl. Descartes despised history, since it lacked the certainty of mathematics and physics. Husserl was hardly interested in history, even the history of philosophy. Philosophy, on his view as on Descartes's, is based on intuitively evident truths that can in principle be discerned at any time. The history of ideas is irrelevant to their truth. The third solution is a 'compromise'—Heidegger associates it with Georg Simmel (1858–1918): it 'acknowledges a minimum of absolute values, but they are embodied in the historical context only in a relative form' (lx. 48).

None of these solutions suits Heidegger. In philosophy, he insists, no compromises will get us to the heart of the matter.

The philosopher is always a 'beginner' (lxi. 13). Nor are there any evident truths discernible without regard to our historical context. Husserl's distinction between 'factuality' and 'validity' is a 'banal platonism' (xvii. 94). It forgets that our present situation, in which we discern whatever truths we do, is steeped in historical tradition. History is not dead and gone, history is what we are (xvii. 114). Hence the contrast between systematic philosophy and history of philosophy is spurious. The history of philosophy essentially concerns the present. We must study it to shed the inadequate categories it has bequeathed to us. Conversely, we must engage in systematic philosophy too, to acquire a fore-having, fore-sight, and fore-conception, enabling us to make sense of the history of philosophy. This applies to history of any kind. I need some prior view of the past to appreciate a historical source, such as a document or a coin (lviii. 204). Historical remnants alone do not make us historians: we must be equipped to see them *as* evidence of some past event. This prior equipment belongs to the present.

Previous philosophers of history—Platonists, Spengler, and compromisers—make three connected mistakes. They neglect the intertwining of the past with the present. They view the historical past only through the eyes of historians, history as pre-packaged by historiography. They neglect Dasein and Dasein's intrinsic historicality. Individual Dasein is dissolved into a culture: 'Rickert says that the human individual in its uniqueness is no more than what it has contributed to cultural values. Here the concept of the individual is conceived purely platonically' (lx. 50). Or into humanity: Dilthey 'persists in the traditional view of history, which I regard as the aesthetic view of history governed by the idea of humanity' (xvii. 92). Once Dasein comes back into its own, we see the continuity between the past and the present. History is the history of past Dasein and its world, not of anonymous cultures or periods quite distinct from our own.

Happening, history, and fate

The word 'history' refers both to events, especially past events, and to the study or narration of events. German has two words corresponding to 'history', *Historie* and *Geschichte*. Both are similarly ambiguous. But Heidegger reserves *Historie* for the study or narration of past events, 'historiography' or 'historiology'. *Geschichte* is used for the history that *Historie* studies, though Heidegger prefers to consider it independently of *Historie*. The words 'historical' (*geschichtlich*) and 'historicality' (*Geschichtlichkeit*) stem from *Geschichte*. Two other words related to *Geschichte* are *Schicksal*, 'fate', and *Geschick*, 'destiny'. But these words, like *Geschichte* itself, derive ultimately from *geschehen*, an ordinary word for 'happen' or 'occur', but often translated as 'historize' in Heidegger's texts, to capture its affinity to *Geschichte*.

How do these seemingly diverse concepts—history, happening, fate—fit together? Let us start with happening or 'historizing'. What *happens*? Dasein *happens*. Dasein stretches out between its birth and its death, and the 'specific movement in which Dasein is stretched along and stretches itself along, we call its "historizing"' (BT, 375). Dasein does not happen as a sequence of momentary experiences borne by a persisting subject. It happens by running ahead to its own death and returning to its birth, by resolutely choosing one of its possibilities in the present 'moment of vision', and by adhering to it in 'self-constancy'. This possibility is Dasein's fate:

> Once one has grasped the finitude of one's existence, it snatches
> one back from the endless multiplicity of possibilities which offer
> themselves as closest to one—those of comfortableness, shirking, and
> taking things lightly—and brings Dasein into the simplicity of its fate.
> (BT, 384)

Only someone who has a fate in this sense can suffer at the hands of fate in the external sense. An irresolute person who drifts with the tide may have bad luck, but cannot suffer the blows of fate. 'Fate' is different from 'destiny':

> But if fateful Dasein, as Being-in-the-world, exists essentially in
> Being with Others, its historizing is a co-historizing and is
> determinative for it as destiny. This is how we designate the
> historizing of the community, of a people.
>
> (BT, 384)

Destiny is not simply the aggregate of the fates of separate individuals. Our fates are orchestrated into a single destiny by our interaction in a common world with a shared history:

> Only in communicating and in struggling does the power of destiny
> become free. Dasein's fateful destiny in and with its 'generation'
> goes to make up the full authentic historizing of Dasein.
>
> (BT, 384f.)

Heidegger steers a course between extreme individualism and complete absorption in the *they*.

'Some talk of Alexander, and some of hercules'

Running ahead to death frees Dasein from the grip of *them* and ensures the authenticity of its resolve. But it does not of itself tell Dasein what to do or even supply it with a range of possibilities for its fate. For this, Dasein must return to the past, perhaps to its own birth, but more likely beyond. There an expanse of possibilities is opened up. There are great philosophers, generals, statesmen, artists, saints, and lovers, whose deeds and works belong to Dasein's heritage. There are also humble sextons like Heidegger's father; heroes come in all shapes and sizes. Dasein should 'repeat' or 'retrieve' such a possibility, it should 'choose its hero' (BT, 385).

Repeating a possibility does not mean reproducing it exactly. I cannot reproduce Alexander's campaigns; I could copy word for word Plato's texts, but this would be both pointless and unplatonic. Repetition is like a conversation with the past or with some past hero. Alexander or Plato make suggestions to me, in their own deeds and works, and I make a rejoinder to them. I thereby disavow 'that which in the "today" is working itself out as the "past"' (BT, 438); I disown the possibilities and interpretations presented to me by *them*.

Dasein's choice of heroes is not unlimited. French revolutionaries tried to emulate ancient rebels and republicans. Napoleon perhaps proposed a rejoinder to Alexander or Caesar. But most people opt for one of the roles handed down from the immediate past—a shoemaker, a priest, a sexton. Heidegger selected his heroes from among philosophers. Aristotle, or perhaps Brentano, who first induced him to become a philosopher rather than a sexton, a priest, or a soldier. Aristotle too guides his attempts to do philosophy, though other philosophers—Plato, Kant, and so on—also come into play.

Dasein need not choose only one hero nor only one type of hero: Heidegger later invokes poets such as Hölderlin and Rilke. He repeats them: he interprets them—armed with his own fore-having, fore-sight, and fore-conception—replies to them, confronting them with the problems and solutions current in his own day, but abandoning or reworking these problems and solutions in view of his engagement with the past. In later works he explicitly presents himself as engaged in a 'conversation' with past thinkers and poets. This is Heidegger's fate. How does it play its part in a destiny? Napoleon's fate is part of the destiny of France. Heidegger's fate belongs to the destinies of progressively wider communities: to the destiny of his pupils and followers, of Freiburg University, of the German people, and perhaps ultimately of what he later called 'the West'. Must Napoleon's followers each have a fate, as well as Napoleon, if France is to have a destiny? Must Heidegger's pupils be as resolute as Heidegger himself, or is it enough if they take his word for it? How many Germans need to be resolutely authentic on their own account? If only it were as easy as Heidegger supposes to distinguish a destiny from *them*!

Inauthentic historicality

Mostly Dasein is not resolute, but it is nevertheless historical. Its historicality differs from that of authentic Dasein in two respects. Firstly, since it does not run ahead to its death and revert to its birth, does not abide in self-constancy by a resolution formed in a moment of vision; it seems more like a series of distinct experiences strung out along a persisting subject. This gives rise to what Heidegger regards as a bogus problem: what is it about these experiences that connects them together as the experiences of a single person? Secondly, irresolute Dasein derives its view of history and the past more from the objects of its daily concern than authentic Dasein does. History becomes world-history.

But 'world-history' is an ambiguous term. In one sense, even authentic historicality is world-history, since what is historical is not solitary Dasein, not a worldless subject, but Dasein in a world. In another sense 'world-history' refers not to the historicality of Dasein, but to the historicality of items within the world—of tools, books, buildings, even nature 'as a countryside, as an area that has been colonized or exploited, as a battlefield, or as the site of a cult' (BT, 388f.). Inauthentic, fallen Dasein is dispersed in the world of the present: 'Lost in the making present of the "today", it understands the "past" in terms of the "Present"' (BT, 391)—not, as authentic Dasein does, in terms of the future, of its own fate.

The meaning of inauthentic historicality becomes clearer if we consider Heidegger's own fate, the practice of philosophy. What does a philosopher do if his existence is inauthentically historical? He may, on the one hand, be a purely 'systematic' philosopher, concerned with current ideas to the exclusion of the history of the subject. 'With the inconstancy of the they-self Dasein makes present its "today". In awaiting the next new thing, it has already forgotten the old one' (BT, 391). He is oblivious to the *history* of current ideas: 'it is loaded down with the legacy of a "past" which has become unrecognizable, and it seeks the modern' (BT, 391). Conversely, an inauthentically historical philosopher may be interested in the history of philosophy, in the texts of past philosophers. An interest in history is no guarantee of authentic historicality. To see why this is so, we need to look at Heidegger's account of 'historiology'.

From historicality to historiology

Dasein is invariably historical, though often only inauthentically historical. Not all Dasein is historiological—interested in the explicit study of history—nor are all ages. Authentic 'historicality does not necessarily require historiology. It is not the case that unhistoriological eras as such are unhistorical also' (BT, 396). Heidegger has in mind the Greeks, who, though they produced the first serious historians—Herodotus and Thucydides—were not so intensely interested in their past as the Romans, let alone 19th-century Germans. They were entitled to neglect the history of philosophy, at least, since they were originators of the subject, free of the burden of tradition that weighs on us. The Greeks made history with more ardour than they studied it.

Nevertheless, historiology is rooted in Dasein's historicality. Historiology, like all sciences, presupposes a prior disclosure of the realm that it 'thematizes'. It also presupposes the present survival of remnants of a past world—documents, buildings, and skeletons. But they will not be treated as historical evidence unless we regard them as 'world-historical':

> Our going back to 'the past' does not first get its start from the acquisition, sifting, and securing of such material; these activities presuppose historical Being towards the Dasein that

has-been-there—that is, they presuppose the historicality of the
historian's existence.

(BT, 394)

Dasein has 'historical Being to the Dasein that has been there' in
that it chooses a role from among those it inherits from the recent
past. But even unhistoriological Dasein is familiar with various
figures and events of the past. We know that Caesar crossed the
Rubicon, even if we do not know why he did so or where the
Rubicon is. When we are making a significant and irrevocable
choice—a choice to marry, say, which though less momentous
than Caesar's, is significant for one's own life—we often regard
ourselves as crossing the Rubicon. We then 'repeat' Caesar's
action. The historian, too, makes choices and may appeal to the
past in making them. If he is, say, a politician, the problems he
faces and the choices he makes in his political life will affect his
selection of a historical theme: 'The "selection" of what is to
become a possible object for historiology has already been met
with in the factical existentiell choice of Dasein's historicality'
(BT, 395). Macaulay's decision to write a history of England from
the accession of James II was influenced by his championship of
the 1831 Reform Bill and of other progressive causes. Augustine's
history of Rome, in the *City of God*, was inspired by Alaric's
sacking of Rome together with his own resolute devotion to
Christianity.

Historiology and Dasein's possibilities

How does an authentically historical historian approach the past?
Dasein exists, it chooses its way of being from the available
possibilities. This is how the historian views himself, and how he
views the past Dasein he studies. He is concerned not simply
with what past Dasein actually did or did not do, but with the
possibilities available, what it could have chosen as well as what it
did choose, and also with the possibilities it hands down to us.
The authentic historian tells us not simply that Caesar crossed the

Rubicon and what resulted from this. He tells us that Caesar faces three possibilities. He can remain in Gaul with his army; then his enemies in Rome will withhold supplies and reinforcements, eventually reducing him to impotence. He can return to Rome without his army; then his enemies will kill him. Or he can illegally cross into Italy with his army; then there will be a civil war.

A statesman or a general might study Caesar's situation for the possibilities that it opens up to himself, for its bearing on his own situation. But again it is easier to see what Heidegger has in mind if we consider the history of philosophy. A philosopher does not simply make certain claims. He makes choices, choosing this possibility rather than that. Descartes responded to scepticism by attempting to rebuild the edifice of knowledge from self-evident premises.

But other responses are possible—that of Montaigne, say, who argued that if everything is uncertain, then Protestantism is uncertain, so that one may as well stick to Catholicism. A reader of Descartes (Kierkegaard, say) may prefer a possibility he neglected. Or a reader (say, Schopenhauer) of Plato's *Republic*, which argues that art lies at two removes from the true forms or Ideas—since it copies ordinary objects which are themselves copies of Ideas—may wonder at Plato's neglect of another possibility—that art directly depicts Ideas.

Again, in the first edition of his *Critique of Pure Reason* Kant broached the possibility that our faculties of sensibility and understanding are both rooted in imagination; in the second edition he abandoned this idea and reinstated the primacy of reason. Heidegger preferred the possibility rejected by Kant, that man is an imaginative being rather than a primarily rational being. (Nevertheless Heidegger disavows *irrationalism*: 'When irrationalism...talks about the things to which rationalism is blind, it does so only with a squint' (BT, 136).) Past philosophers are to be read with a view to their possibilities—possibilities chosen, rejected, suppressed, but all left to us.

Nietzsche's possibilities

In the second of his *Untimely Meditations*, 'On the Use and Abuse of History for Life' (1874), Nietzsche distinguished three types of historiology: the monumental (which portrays the glories of the past as an inspiration to the present and future), the antiquarian (recording the past for its own sake), and the critical (which censures the blemishes of the past). Why just three possibilities? And are they alternatives? Nietzsche, Heidegger suggests, 'understood more than he has made known to us' (BT, 396), and in view of Dasein's temporality all three are involved in authentic historiology. As resolutely futural, Dasein is 'open for the "monumental" possibilities of human existence' (BT, 396), and this gives rise to monumental historiology. But since Dasein is also 'thrown', it has the 'possibility of reverently preserving the existence that has-been-there', the existence which revealed to it the possibility it has chosen.

This is antiquarian historiology. Dasein also has to make its choice in the present, but not the present as *they* interpret it. Authentic historiology is 'a way of painfully detaching oneself from the falling publicness of the "today"', and so, as well as being monumental and antiquarian, it is also a 'critique of the "Present"' (BT, 397). Nietzsche, read in the right way, confirms Heidegger's account of history.

Dasein which has been there

Nietzsche was dead when BT appeared. So was Descartes, and many other philosophers Heidegger considered. Husserl (1859–1938) was still alive. Yet Heidegger treats Husserl much as he does Descartes: they are both 'possibilities of the being of care' (xvii. 107). Does it matter to historicality whether other Dasein are dead or alive? Sometimes Heidegger suggests that it does. Artefacts are historical because they were 'used by a concernful Dasein who was-in-the-world. That world is no longer' (BT, 280). Hence historiology deals with Dasein that has been there, and, since

Dasein is Being-in-the-world, that involves world-history: 'If Dasein is there no longer, then the world too is something that has-been-there' (BT, 393).

Dasein's world dies along with Dasein, Heidegger implies. This is puzzling. Two contemporaries are each in-the-world. But they are in the same world. Why can I not be in the same world as someone was who is now dead? Moreover, contemporaries do not conveniently die at the same time, nor need they all be dead before we write the history of their exploits: there are still survivors of World War II. We should distinguish 'having been there' from 'being no longer there'.

What matters to Heidegger as a historical being is that Husserl has been there: Husserl's texts were ('always already') on hand from his schooldays, like those of Descartes. It makes no difference from this point of view, though it may from others, that Husserl is still around, available for questioning and ready to answer back, while Descartes is not.

Can Dasein's historicality sustain the idea of an objective temporal order, in which Descartes lived and died before the birth of Kant, who in turn died before Husserl was born? As Heidegger scans the pages of Descartes he finds no mention of Kant or Husserl, whereas Husserl refers often to Descartes and Kant. Were they each in a different world? This is less plausible with regard to their thought than other aspects of their life. Kant's philosophy is less outmoded than his wig. But to place them in chronological order, and give the dates of their births and deaths, we need to assign them to the same world and the same world-time.

World-time

Time is 'significant'. Dasein needs time for doing things, it takes time to do things, it can 'lose' or waste time. This depends on Dasein's being as care, its temporality, and its finitude:

> The 'there' is disclosed in a way which is grounded in Dasein's own temporality as ecstatically stretched along, and with this disclosure a 'time' is allotted to Dasein; only because of this can Dasein, as factically thrown, 'take' its time and lose it.
>
> (BT, 410)

The *significance* of time is more fundamental than time-reckoning or time-measurement. I look at my watch because I need to get to a meeting on time. I consult my diary because I wonder whether I shall meet my deadline. I would not consult watches or diaries if I did not need time to do things, if I did not need to do things on time.

Corresponding to the three ecstases there are three temporal adverbs: 'then' (*dann*) referring to a future time, 'now' (*jetzt*) referring to the present, and 'then' or 'on that former occasion' (*damals*) referring to a past time. We use these in planning: I must dress *now* before the cab arrives *then*; I must resit the exam which I failed *then* on that former occasion. Both 'then' and 'on that former occasion' involve 'now'; 'then' implies 'now-not-yet', and 'on that former occasion' implies 'now-no-longer'; the cab is not yet here, and I am not failing my exam *now*. Temporality 'ensnares itself in the Present, which, in making present, says pre-eminently "Now! Now!"' (BT, 407).

The 'now', 'then', and 'on that former occasion' are 'datable'. We assign a time to worldly events: 'then, when the cab arrives', 'now that you are dressed', 'then, when you failed the exam'. This is related to time's significance: we could not plan our activities temporally, unless we could assign times to them. Time is also 'spanned' or extended. We refer not primarily to instants but to the time in-between: 'I'll read until the cab comes', 'I've worked ever since I failed the exam'. Even the present is not a durationless instant, but a shorter or longer span of time: '"now"—in the intermission, while one is eating, in the evening, in summer'

(BT, 409). This is related to datability. What we do, and what happens, takes time—we cannot do anything in a durationless instant. Time is public. This too is related to datability. Often we date the same time by different events. The time that for me is *then*, *when* I married is for you *then*, *when* you left school. But usually we manage to date a time by an event known to us both: I married, and you left school, *then*, *when* England last won the World Cup. We coordinate our actions in public time: we arrange to meet *then*, *when* the concert ends.

Life is made easier by clocks. The natural, primeval clock is the sun, by whose light we see to perform our daily tasks. The sun is there for everyone in the same longitude. It is not attached to any particular person or business. We measure time, initially, by the positions of the sun: 'because the temporality of the Dasein which must take its time is finite, its days are already numbered' (BT, 413). We measure time because there is a right time and a wrong time for doing things. Like the world, time is *significant*. Hence time becomes worldly, world-time, a time within which everything present-at-hand or ready-to-hand has its place. Later, when we become less dependent on sunlight for our activities, we devise clocks that do not require sunlight—though they must keep in time, more or less, with the sun.

'Ordinary time'

Measurement, as it becomes more refined, alters our conception of time. It stresses the present at the expense of the other ecstases. A runner in a race does not focus primarily on the present. He looks ahead to the moment when he will cross the finishing line to the applause of the spectators. He gears himself up for the final sprint. All this is lost on the person timing his run. *Now*, at 3 o'clock by his watch, the runner sets off; *now*, at 3.05, he is half-way; *now*, at 3.10, he crosses the finishing line. The timer is not wholly oblivious to the past and the future. He 'retains' the start of the run at 3.00, and awaits its completion. But retention and waiting are muffled by the imperious presence of the now.

Time measured is still spanned. The race *lasts* 10 minutes, from 3.00 to 3.10. But the *now* is not spanned. The race begins at exactly 3.00, not in a long-drawn-out now, as when a spectator says 'It's going to begin now'. And it ends at exactly 3.10. The present of time-measurement is, ideally at least, not spanned.

Time is still public and still significant. I am timing a runner, and the time of his run is articulated by its phases; the time, like the run, has a beginning, a middle, and an end. Other spectators see the race and their watches, perhaps, say the same as mine. But the time-measurer is more engrossed in the movements of his watch, and less in events in the world, than the runner or an excited spectator. In periods of boredom clocks can take complete control. As I wait for a train in an empty station, time seems empty and homogeneous, punctuated by nothing except the movements of the clock. It is related to no significant events; it seems to be an entity in its own right.

This, Heidegger argues, gives rise to Aristotle's view of time, as a sequence of nows. Shorn of its datability and significance, ecstatic temporality gets 'levelled off' (BT, 422), so that time is homogeneous. The nows are seen as present-at-hand, and time is almost a thing among other things. Now-time is uninterrupted and has no gaps—unlike ecstatic temporality, which glides over periods in which nothing is happening. It is infinite—a feature Heidegger attributes to 'fleeing in the face of death' (BT, 424). It is thoroughly public: it 'belongs to everybody—and that means, to nobody' (BT, 425).

Nevertheless, now-time retains marks of its origin in temporality. Time is said to pass away, rather than to arise: 'Dasein knows fugitive time in terms of its "fugitive" knowledge about its death' (BT, 425). It is also irreversible, moving irrevocably in one direction, and this can be explained only by its derivation from ecstatic temporality. It makes little difference to the timer of the race if the race runs backwards, or even if his watch runs backwards; he can still time the race. But it cannot be so for the runner himself, looking ahead to the finishing line, with victory in his grasp but not yet fully assured. Now-time, then, derives from ecstatic temporality. Conversely, it would be difficult, perhaps impossible, to construct ecstatic temporality out of impoverished now-time, however much we plaster it over with significance and value.

Now-time is derivative. It does not follow that it is unreal or illegitimate: 'The ordinary representation of time has its natural justification' (BT, 426). Historiology requires world-time, if not now-time: 'Temporality temporalizes world-time, within the horizon of which "history" can "appear" as historizing within-time' (BT, 436). Heidegger does not discard world-time in favour of ecstatic temporality. That would eliminate the stable framework within which resoluteness operates. Authenticity, resoluteness, ecstatic temporality—these enable me to grapple with the texts of Aristotle and to propose, say, that the original meaning of 'truth' was 'unconcealment'. Inauthenticity, fallenness, world-time—these enable me to speak contemporary English and to say that Aristotle died in 322 BCE. Here as elsewhere inauthenticity serves its purpose.

Heidegger versus Hegel

In the penultimate section of BT, Heidegger argues that Hegel (1770–1831) accepted Aristotle's conception of time and did not go far beyond it. Why Hegel? In part it is because Heidegger had immense respect for Hegel,

> who saw and was able to see in philosophy so much more than had
> ever been seen before, because he had an uncommon power over
> language and wrested concealed things from their hiding-places.
>
> (xxiv. 226)

In part it is because Hegel seems to anticipate some of Heidegger's doctrines and strategies. Hegel's *Phenomenology of Spirit* (1807) can readily be seen as a rejection of traditional epistemology in favour of ontology, an exploration of the being of the knower and the known, and of the relationship between them. But Heidegger won't have it. For him Hegel is the last and greatest of the Cartesians; the supreme rationalist, who dissolved ontology into logic; the overweening metaphysician, who saw man as infinite, destined to view reality through the eye of God. So Heidegger takes issue with Hegel—both to remove a monstrous obstacle on the path to truth and to make sure that no one confuses Heidegger with Hegel.

One trait Heidegger shares with Hegel is a tendency not to finish the books he promised to write. Hegel's *Phenomenology* was originally published as the first part of a system, to be followed by a second part on logic, nature, and mind. This second part never appeared. Heidegger undoubtedly knew this when he left BT incomplete, but kept the words 'First Half' on the title-page until 1953. Did he hope to invite comparison between Hegel's *Phenomenology* and his own BT, the one recording the voyage of consciousness (*Bewusstsein*) through various 'forms', the other exploring ever-deeper levels of Dasein's Being, behind the masks of its self-interpretations?

No doubt we should suggest some more substantial reason for Heidegger's failure to continue BT. He ends with the question 'Does time itself manifest itself as the horizon of Being?' (BT, 437). His idea seems to be that our new understanding of time enables us to consider Being in general, disregarding its particular modes and its relationship to Dasein. More than once he indicates that Dasein can only be analysed properly if 'the ontology of possible entities within-the-world is oriented securely enough by clarifying the idea of Being in general' (BT, 366). Does BT leave much of interest to be said about this? It is not obvious that we need to elucidate Being in general to understand the differences between various modes of Being—between rocks, tools, Dasein, time, and world.

Heidegger regards Being in general as a 'horizon' for differentiating modes of Being, a vantage point beyond any particular type of entity from which we can survey and discriminate their varieties and interrelations. But even if finite Dasein can attain such a vantage point, what might there be of interest to find once it gets there? Moreover, Heidegger seems to have closed off the route to Dasein-independent Being, or to a vantage point beyond Dasein itself, by his persistent claim that there is no Being *without* Dasein. BT has not focused on the Being of Dasein to the exclusion of other entities. Time, world, hammers, rocks—all these are interpreted by Dasein in their Being. What more can there be to Being than what Dasein makes of all this?

However, Heidegger's thought did not end with BT. Often he seems to contradict BT, and sometimes protests that it was misunderstood: it was not his aim 'to show that the essence of man consists in handling a spoon and fork, and travelling by tram' (xxix–xxx, 263). It needs no special explanation that in his long literary career Heidegger did not continually rework the same themes and occasionally changed his mind. What is remarkable, and testifies to his 'resoluteness', is his attempt to integrate all his work into a single coherent whole. A brief, and inevitably selective, survey of Heidegger's thought after BT will reveal something of the overall coherence of his lifelong project.

Chapter 10
After *Being and Time*

Apart from complaints about chatter and curiosity, BT gave
a fairly favourable account of the world in which we live.
The history of this world intrudes into our present in the relics
left by past generations. These enable us to revive our past history
and use it to guide our choices and decisions. The philosopher,
too, studies the past history of his discipline in order to guide his
choices and gain resources for analysing this world and Dasein's
place in it. But this leaves a question unanswered: how was such
a world established in the first place? This question acquired
additional urgency from Heidegger's realization that the modern
world is not as benign as it looked in 1927. Have there been
better worlds in the past and, if so, what is the nature of, and the
reason for, the decline? Is there any prospect of a return to our
earlier condition?

To answer these questions Heidegger turned to something barely
mentioned in BT: art. His first exhibit, Van Gogh's painting of
peasant shoes, conveys the idea that shoes are not simply things
for walking, but invoke the world of the peasant, and the earth
on which they are planted, in a way that no actual shoes,
inconspicuous as shoes usually are, can do (see Figure 9). Van
Gogh reveals an existing world; he does not establish a world
afresh. Heidegger's next exhibit repairs this deficiency: a Greek
temple not only reveals a world, but sets it up, wresting from

9. Shoes, a painting by van Gogh.

the earth a world in which the Greek people could live
(see Figure 10). But humans need above all a language in order
to comprehend their world and this was supplied by Heidegger's
final exhibit, poetry. Tragedies and the epics of Homer and
Hesiod gave Greeks words enabling them to make sense of their
world and themselves. It gave them a new conception of *Being*.

This raises a problem. Within an *established* world, it is Dasein
that makes choices, uses words, and occasionally coins words.
Accordingly, in BT Being was subordinate to Dasein; there
could be no Being without Dasein. But in the work of *establishing*
a world, Dasein cannot play this part: it lacks a culture and
language adequate for the decisions required.

World-forming must therefore be the work not of Dasein, but
of Being itself, and Dasein thus becomes subordinate to Being.

10. The Parthenon, the temple of Athena on the Athenian Acropolis, 438 BCE.

Dasein is nevertheless the 'shepherd of Being' and poets are sometimes described as demigods, standing in a no man's land between gods and humanity, transmitting the hints of the gods to the people. It is in this no man's land that it is decided who man is and where he establishes his existence (HEP).

Poets cannot do their work in any normal human way, since that would presuppose the world yet to be established. They must be the vehicle of an impersonal force—art or truth or Being itself. The foundation of a world is a mystery, an 'original leap'. The history of art, and of humanity as a whole, is not a steady cumulative process, but punctuated by massive explosions of creative energy, altering our whole conception of Being. Such explosions come, if anywhere, from Being itself.

There have been three such explosions in the West: first, and most radically, in Greece, with its conception of Being as 'presence'; second, in medieval times, when beings were conceived as entities created by God, as existences corresponding to their essences in

116

the divine mind. And finally in modern 'technology', where beings have become 'objects', to be calculated and manipulated. History is now primarily the history of Being.

Heidegger concedes that art plays no such crucial role in the second and third of these transformations as it did in Greece. He admits other ways of staking a claim to 'truth', such as a political constitution, though he denies such a role to science: science is not an 'original happening of truth'. It fills in the details of a 'domain of truth already opened ... [I]nsofar as a science passes beyond correctness and goes on to a truth, ... it is philosophy.' (OWA 62).

Here we encounter two surprises. The first is the jaundiced characterization of the modern world; it is now a far cry from the folksy world of the village shoemaker described in BT. The second is the implied suggestion that philosophy itself plays a part in these cultural explosions and is not simply a way of describing them.

The solutions to these two problems are interconnected. One feature of BT's account of the world is its rejection of certain traditional terms for describing it, notably 'subject', 'object', and 'idea' or 'representation', primarily because they assume a gulf between ourselves and the world: we are not self-enclosed knowing 'subjects' reaching out to 'objects'; our access to things is direct, not mediated by a screen of 'ideas' or sensations.

Later, wrenched away from the cosy Black Forest by Nazism and war, Heidegger decides that after all the modern world is aptly conceptualized in terms of 'subjects' relating to 'objects' by way of 'representations'. Dasein is no longer properly Dasein, but a subject, using its representations of objects to calculate and manipulate them. Thus philosophers have supplied a vocabulary for describing technology. Are philosophers responsible for technology? Is technology not a matter of machines, and thus

the responsibility of scientists and entrepreneurs? But, insists
Heidegger, technology is not primarily machines. It is a mindset,
a way of looking at the world—as a stock of exploitable resources.
It is not just a way of making or doing things, but a way of
revealing things that precedes the making: 'That there is such a
thing as e.g. a diesel engine has its decisive, ultimate ground
in the fact that the categories of a "nature" utilizable by machine
technology were once specifically thought and thought through by
philosophers' (NII, 76/iv, 39). Technology engulfs and diminishes
the world, threatening to turn man from a Being-in-the-world
into a 'mechanized animal', treating us all as exploitable human
resources. It results in a world whose human significance is
flattened out, where we are rootless and no longer at home.

Technology is the 'completion of metaphysics'. In writings of the
BT period, 'metaphysics' is a favourable term, roughly equivalent
to the 'ontology' Heidegger espoused. By the late 1930s it became
derogatory, primarily because it denotes anthropocentric,
man-centred philosophy that regards the truth of and about
beings as depending on human ideas and values, and is therefore
'forgetful of Being'. (Despite Heidegger's denial, BT might well
be suspected of metaphysics in *this* sense.)

This metaphysics was, in Heidegger's view, inaugurated by Plato,
whose cave allegory in the *Republic* brought truth 'under the yoke
of the *idea*', thereby transforming it from 'unhiddenness' into
mere 'correctness', i.e. *our* ideas in correspondence to things.
This man-centred metaphysics was inherited by Descartes,
who restricted what there is to what *we* can be certain of. Finally
there is Nietzsche, the 'most unbridled Platonist in the history
of Western metaphysics'. 'Truth', Nietzsche said, 'is the sort of
error without which a definite type of living entity could not live.
Ultimately, the value for life decides.' This is 'metaphysical',
because it locates truth in our thought; it is 'Platonist', because it
assumes a realm of values distinct from the world. Nietzsche

confirms the 'forgetfulness of Being', the 'nihilism' that has culminated in technology.

None of this entails that philosophers freely and deliberately gave rise to technology or even to metaphysics itself. Technology is sent to us by Being, to which metaphysical philosophers themselves are in thrall. Philosophers, like artists, are not in control of their own products, but in the grip of an impersonal force. The only philosophers innocent of metaphysics are such 'Presocratic' thinkers as Anaximander, Parmenides, and Heraclitus. So Heidegger scours their obscure and fragmentary texts for anticipations of his own view and for clues as to how metaphysics and forgetfulness of being might be overcome: 'Language speaks, not man. Man only speaks when he fatefully answers to language' (PR 96).

Presocratic philosophers usually wrote in poetic language. Language was one of Heidegger's abiding interests, but his view of language, and his own use of language, passed through three phases. In his earliest writings he accepted Husserl's view that language expresses a system of meaning that is essentially extra-linguistic, independent of any particular language, of our psychological states, and of the contexts in which sentences are uttered. This language is not especially poetic. Metaphor and ambiguity are avoided and words have clear, stable meanings. Words should express our thoughts, not intrude so as to provoke or alter our thoughts.

In the early 1920s, culminating in BT, Heidegger shed the 'banal Platonism' of Husserl's 'theoretical attitude'. Grammar is to be liberated from 'logic'. Language no longer expresses a timeless web of meaning, but is rooted in human activity. This does not reinstate 'psychologism': we are now Dasein, beings-in-the world, not receptacles of mental events. Language is based on informal *talk* in a particular context. It need not involve a grammatically complete sentence. It need not be an assertion. 'Fire!' is a kind of talk, so is a request, such as 'Another one, please!'

On the earlier view, what matters is the speaker and the meaning, not the hearer. But talk needs a hearer; a listener is also talking. So talk involves silence too. We are not really talking if we both talk at once. Silence is as pregnant as words. Language is not primary; prior to talk, logically if not temporally, is our understanding of the world and its significance, and our interpretations of particular entities: 'Talk is the articulation of intelligibility.' Talk is not yet language: language emerges from talk when it breaks free of particular contexts and gets repeated by others in a disengaged manner. The worldly significance that we already understand enables us to form 'meanings', and so gives rise to words and language.

'Untrue', protests Heidegger in a marginal note to BT. 'Language is not superimposed; it *is* the original essence of truth as There.' This is his third view of language. It accompanies a change in his conception of the world. In BT the world is a familiar realm of interwoven significance. Now he conceives the world as 'beings as a whole'. Beings as a whole have no ready-made significance. How is a significant world, fit for human habitation, first established? It is done by words, both basic words, such as *phusis*, the Greek for 'nature', that open up a view of things as a whole, and more specific words that lay foundations for a particular form of life. Words gather phenomena into stable, persisting entities; they create an open space of entities for us to deal with and talk about, and thus create speakers and hearers. Such words are formed by inspired poets rather than reflective philosophers. Language is now the 'house of being'.

Heidegger's concern is no longer only the language of his own significant world, let alone a logical structure of meaning common to all times and places. He becomes aware of diverse worlds, diverse conceptions of beings as a whole, with corresponding differences in words and language. Our world is not that of ancient Greece, of medieval Christianity, or of modern Japan, and our language too differs from theirs.

Heidegger's own use of language changes along with his general view of language. Early on, it is ordinary philosophical language. In BT it is still somewhat scholastic, though with some peculiar features. He exploits the etymology of the words he uses and their connexions with each other. Language opens up and orders the world for us. It reveals aspects of the world of which we are usually unaware. Heidegger relishes ambiguity and change of meaning, supposing them to disclose deep truths about reality:

> 'The Dasein in man *forms* [*bildet*] the world' means: 1. it establishes it, 2. it pictures it, 3. it constitutes, circumscribes it.... If we speak of world-forming in this threefold sense, is that play with language? Certainly, more precisely it is playing along with the play of language. This play of language is not playful; it springs from a lawfulness that precedes all 'logic' and makes deeper demands on us than does following the rules of definition-formation. [...] we must dare to play this game in order to [...] escape the spell of everyday talk and its concepts.
>
> (xxix–xxx, 414)

Heidegger's language is more dynamic than standard philosophical language. He prefers verbs and vigorous adjectives to substance-words. He replaces 'man' with the verbal 'Dasein', and 'space' and 'time' with 'spatial(ity)' and 'temporal(ity)'. Heidegger likes to draw distinctions, to apply different words to different types of entity. Bertrand Russell uses the same notation for the existence of different types of thing. Hammers, electrons, and humans all exist and they exist in the same ways. For Heidegger they have different types of being and we must find words to express these differences.

In later writings Heidegger's language becomes less scholastic and more poetic. He abandons some of his earlier technical vocabulary and turns to ordinary, albeit poetical language. He now believes that language, like the world as a whole, is suffering from the technological mindset. This is true even of philosophical language: 'metalinguistics is the metaphysics of the thoroughgoing mechanization of all languages exclusively into the operative instrument of interplanetary information. Metalanguage and sputnik, metalinguistics and missile technology are the same' (OWL, 58). The salvation of language is poetry rather than philosophy: 'Language is the original poetry in which a people poetizes Being' (IM, 144)

Inspired by poets such as Hölderlin and Rilke, Heidegger attempted to rescue *things* from the toils of technology and the bureaucratic language it spawns. In standard philosophy a thing is regarded as detached from other things, and as an object of contemplation rather than of use; as H. H. Price remarked, 'When I see a tomato there is much that I can doubt.' For Heidegger a single thing brings the whole world into play. This is expressed in Van Gogh's picture. Indeed, the systematic interrelatedness of things is a persistent theme of BT itself, though BT does not encourage us to focus on a particular thing in the way that a painter or poet may. In later writings Heidegger moves further in this direction.

In BT the two poles of Heidegger's universe were Dasein and world. In OWA another factor comes into play: *earth*. The newly emerging world is engaged in a conflict with the earth from which it is wrested and on which it rests. Finally, the world is conceived as the 'eventful mirror-play' of *four* 'regions': earth, sky, gods, and mortals (T). A thing, such as a jug, a bridge, or a cricket-bat, lies at the intersection of this fourfold: 'The jug is a thing insofar as it things. [...] By thinging, it detains a while earth and sky, the divinities and the mortals; by detaining, the thing brings the four close to each other in their distances.' (As often happens, Heidegger converts a noun into a verb; a thing does its own thing: what it is can be expressed only by a verb of its own.) A cricket-bat is planted on the earth beneath a sky that sheds light and warmth; the weather is a godsend; the success of the stroke is in the lap of the gods. In descriptions of this type Heidegger hoped to extricate things from the clutches of technology and restore the vision of the early Greeks.

> Just as an erotic person is always erotic in nature, whether or not he has found—or ever will find—an object of love, so too a religious person is always religious, whether or not he believes in a God.
>
> (Georg Simmel)

In later writings, Heidegger often mentions 'gods'. What, if any, were his religious beliefs? He excludes theology and religious faith from BT, believing that the idea of a Christian philosophy is as absurd as that of a Christian mathematics. Some of the concepts in BT, such as existence, falling, transcendence, and guilt, are acknowledged to be secularized versions of Christian concepts, and could provide a basis for theology—which is, in Heidegger's view, a distinct science studying religious faith. However, such transformations of religious concepts might equally be attempts to disarm faith of its most potent weapons. Moreover, his claim that Newton's laws were not *true* before Newton disclosed them seems incompatible with the reality of an all-knowing God.

Nevertheless, even in this period, Heidegger does not commit to atheism. What he rejects is the wrong sort of God, the view that God is *a being* alongside others: it is 'better to swallow the cheap accusation of atheism, which in any case, if intended ontically, is fully justified. But is not the supposed ontical faith in God at bottom godlessness?' (xxvi, 211 n.3) and 'man is not the image of God as the absolute petit-bourgeois; this god is the fake product of man' (xxxi, 136). This leaves open the possibility that God is Being itself. But how can that be so, if Being depends on Dasein, as BT suggests?

However, this has changed by 1947, when Heidegger published his 'Letter on Humanism' (LH). 'Man first of all exists, encounters himself, surges up in the world—and defines himself afterwards.... man is nothing other than what he makes of himself.' This sounds like BT. But its author was Jean-Paul Sartre, in his 1946 lecture 'Existentialism and Humanism'. In Sartre's view, man, whether individually or collectively, *makes himself.* Herein lies the most conspicuous difference between Sartre, the self-proclaimed existentialist, and Heidegger, who disclaimed this title. For Heidegger, man is not his own master, but at the beck and call of Being. Sartre relieves God of one of his primary traditional functions and Sartre was also an atheist.

Was Heidegger an atheist? He says not. In BT, Being's dependence on Dasein disqualifies Being for the role of God. But now Dasein is demoted and Being is more godlike. So was he a theist? He denies this too. Heidegger had a chequered religious career: born as a Catholic, he became a Lutheran, then a Nazi, and finally returned to a Catholic graveyard. He often speaks, in later writings, of God and gods, but steadfastly denies that Being is God, primarily because while God is regarded (especially by Aquinas) as a being or entity, Being is not *a* being; it is that in virtue of which there are any beings at all.

In LH he insists, however, that BT did not exclude God's existence: 'With the existential determination of the essence of man...nothing is decided about the "existence of God" or his "non-being", no more than about the possibility of gods.' BT's concept of human 'transcendence' lays the foundation for an adequate account of God: 'through an illumination of transcendence we first achieve an *adequate concept of human being*, with respect to which it can now be asked how the relationship of human being to God is ontologically ordered' (LH, quoting from ER (1929)).

We are not just focused on the thing in front of us that captures our attention at the moment, we are always aware of the larger context in which such things lie—the world around us, and then the wider world beyond. We *transcend*, not only to this or that being, but to beings as a whole and even to Being itself. This secular transcendence underlies our capacity to be 'towards God', to have *faith*, our possible transcendence to a transcendent God. Being 'towards God' depends on Being in general.

Faith is not an attempt to explain the universe. It stems from an experience of the holy, the numinous, the sacredness felt in the presence of certain places, things, persons, or actions. Heidegger fears that modern life with its 'technology' and 'machination' is sapping our sense of the holy: 'Only from the truth of Being can the essence of the holy be thought. Only from the essence of the holy is the essence of the divine to be thought.... Perhaps what is distinctive about this world-epoch consists in the closure of the dimension of the holy. Perhaps that is the only *unholy malignancy*' (LH).

It is hard to say whether Heidegger is a theist, an atheist, or neither, not least in view of his conviction that truth is 'unconcealment' rather than correspondence. Perhaps his view can be summarized like this: we need God or gods. But they are not Being, nor Aquinas's 'God'. They are historically variable manifestations of Being. The gods died with the Greek city state, though poets and scholars intermittently revive them. The God of Christianity is, as Nietzsche said, now dead or dying, killed off by, and partly responsible for, the metaphysics and technology that threaten humanity. To survive this danger we shall, like every preceding age, need a new god or gods—the number is yet to be decided (lxv, 437)—'the last god, quite different from the gods of the past, especially the christian god' (lxv, 403. Cf. xxxix, 93ff.).

Heidegger has hardly any idea whether God or gods exist or not, or whether we will come to believe in them again, or what they will be like if we do come to believe in them. Whether God(s) come again is up to Being, not to us. But he does think that there is a space, a dimension, in which God or gods can be located, and that we are open to this dimension:

> Man does not decide whether and how beings appear, whether and how God and the gods or history and nature come forward into the clearing of Being, come to presence and depart. The advent of beings lies in the destiny of Being. But for man it is ever a question of finding what is fitting in his essence that corresponds to such destiny; for in accord with this destiny man as ek-sisting has to guard the truth of Being. Man is the shepherd of Being.
>
> (LH, 234)

Heidegger hopes that Being will assign him a role in promoting this revival. The effects of technology, as he describes them—homelessness, rootlessness, the flattening out of worldly significance—are similar to the effects he earlier attributed to *Angst* and boredom, moods especially conducive to philosophy. Technology is double-edged. If we succumb to it, it threatens to turn us into the calculating functionaries that he found in the dystopian works of his friend Ernst Jünger. If we think about it in the right way, it offers an unprecedented prospect of philosophical illumination. How else can Heidegger explain how he, in this benighted age, succeeded in recovering the vision of the Greeks?

Chapter 11
St Martin of Messkirch?

Heidegger was a committed Nazi, not an opportunistic Nazi. Despite growing disillusionment, he did not, and probably could not, resign from the party. Nevertheless, he need not have been anti-Semitic. Nazism offered other attractions: anti-communism, traditional values, restoration of German greatness, and relief from the ravages of 'technology'. His published writings, even his rectoral address, contain no overt antisemitism. His relations with Jewish pupils, such as Arendt and Elisabeth Blochmann, were cordial and often amorous. He dedicated books to Husserl and Scheler, both of Jewish descent. As rector of Freiberg he, perforce, fired Jews and anti-Nazis, but helped some to emigrate.

However, scrutiny of Heidegger's life and writings—a closer inspection than most lives receive—has revealed expressions of antisemitism where officialdom did not require them, albeit the conspiratorial rather than biological variety. In a letter of October 1929 he wrote: 'We are faced with a choice, either to provide our German intellectual life once more with real talents and educators rooted in our own soil (*bodenständige*), or to hand over that intellectual life once and for all to the growing judaization (*Verjudung*) in the broad and the narrow sense.' Heidegger's *Black Notebooks*, containing reflections written between 1931 and 1941, seem to confirm his antisemitism. Jews are attributed with a special 'talent for calculation'—a type of thinking that includes such disparate practices as formal logic, statistics, cost-benefit analysis and double-entry bookkeeping. Jews lack a native soil and a world in which they are at home. They are therefore complicit in the domination of 'technology' and the consequent 'rootlessness'—though Americanism, Bolshevism, and even fascism itself also share the blame.

One complaint implies that Jews projected their own faults onto others: 'With their emphatically calculative talent, the Jews have already "lived" the longest according to the race principle, which is why [*weshalb*] they also resist most vehemently its unrestricted application' (BN, XII, 38). Jews opposed Nazi laws prohibiting marriages and sexual relations between Jews and gentiles, not *despite* their own endogamy, but *because of* it. Psychological projection undoubtedly occurs, whether the explanation is (as Freud believed) that we cope with our own faults by casting them off onto others or, alternatively, that the effort of suppressing our faults makes them especially conspicuous to us so that we see them in others, or that we all tend to regard others as similar to ourselves.

There is no evidence that Jews are especially prone to projection. But someone was, and that was Heidegger himself. He is projecting his own projectionism onto others. He reveals his projectionism in a note from 1941: 'World Judaism, incited by the émigrés let go [*herausgelassenen*] from Germany, is everywhere elusive and in the unfolding of its power it does not need to get involved in military action anywhere, whereas we are left to sacrifice the best blood of the best of our people' (BN, XV, 17). Jews do not fight, Heidegger implies. But many Jews did fight and others participated in the intelligence operations that were doubtless too calculative to figure in Heidegger's gung-ho romantic view of warfare. Yet someone did not fight, and that was Heidegger himself. In World War I, he was declared unfit for combat and given a safe desk job. In later writings he often mentions soldiers and their 'authentic' and 'resolute' 'being towards death', which suggests that this safe haven, while friends and compatriots died in battle, left a lifelong burden of guilt.

Heidegger tried to relieve Germany, and himself, of a greater burden of guilt by reworking the trope that Jews were responsible for their own destruction. The Holocaust was not the fault of its perpetrators but of 'technology', the impersonal calculative, exploitative mindset impelling us to factory-farm chickens as well as gas Jews. Since Jews play a significant part in technology, if anyone is responsible for their annihilation, it is Jews themselves. The blame is shifted onto the victims.

Heidegger's references to 'rootlessness' present a more interesting case of projection. He reportedly said in a seminar: 'From the specific knowledge of a people about the nature of its space, we first experience how nature is revealed in this people. For a Slavic people, the nature of our German space would definitely be revealed differently from the way it is revealed to us; to Semitic nomads it will perhaps never be revealed at all' (NHS, 56).

Jews were well integrated into German society and not especially rootless. If anyone was rootless it was Heidegger himself. Born into a conservative Catholic community with deep roots in the soil of the Black Forest, and educated by the Church, he became a Jesuit novice, but was discharged, owing to the heart defect that later exempted him from the battlefield. From then on, he tore up his roots. He switched from theology to philosophy. He married a Protestant in a Catholic ceremony, then a Protestant one. His marriage was open and he had many affairs. He renounced the 'system of Catholicism' and effectively became a Lutheran. As if to compensate for his apostasy, he clung tenaciously to his roots. He affected peasant clothes and manners. He spurned offers of a chair in Berlin, preferring to work in his mountain-side hut, which he insisted was especially conducive to philosophical thought. Spiritually, however, Heidegger wandered as far as the legendary eternal Jew.

Rootlessness plays an important part in Heidegger's thought. He links rootlessness with 'technology', the capitalist mindset, and Jews with capitalism as well as with Bolshevism—which he regarded as another version of technology. Capitalism and communism are both cosmopolitan. They promote speed of travel and communication, railways and radio in Heidegger's day, aeroplanes, television, and the internet in ours. They thereby flatten or homogenize the world and alienate us from our native environment.

However, philosophy itself requires a certain detachment. For Heidegger, it was important to appreciate one's local space, 'our German space', the up–down, right–left, here–there everyday space in which German peasants measured time and distance by pipefuls smoked on a journey. Newton, Descartes, and Einstein were less concerned about this space than the space of science, which is not even space for everyday humans, let alone for peasants. But a deeply rooted German peasant would not have a better understanding of everyday space than Newton, Descartes, or Einstein. He may know what his space is like and, more generally, what it is like to be a German peasant. But since he would not know what it is like *not* to be a German peasant, he could not make his understanding explicit or communicate it in an articulate manner. As soon as he can do this, he is no longer an ordinary peasant.

A philosopher may have one foot planted in the Black Forest, but his other foot must be planted elsewhere. Heidegger knew this, but he rejected his predecessors' recipes for attaining such a posture. Descartes ascended to an appropriate distance from the everyday world by doubting the existence of everything except his own ego, and Husserl conducted a quasi-Cartesian

Epoche, a suspension of belief in everything except the contents of his own consciousness.

However, Heidegger regarded such moves as inadequately motivated and stemming from a strange, and philosophically misguided, 'concern for certainty'. Why, he wondered, should an ordinary human being ever become a philosopher? His answer is that everyday life itself contains the beginnings from which, if suitably nurtured, the philosophical attitude will germinate.

We all occasionally experience anxiety and boredom. Most of us let these moods pass and make nothing of them. Not so Heidegger. In BT and subsequent lectures, he argued that a philosopher should cultivate such moods, which flatten everything out and make it seem strange and uncanny, dislodging his secure foothold in the here and now and leaving him thereafter at a certain distance from previously familiar things. Heidegger believes that a groundbreaking philosopher, such as he purported to be, is even more removed from the familiar. He remains aloof from the everyday world of philosophy—conferences, peer-reviewed journals, and research assessment exercises. He spends time with such ancients as Aristotle, Plato, and Heraclitus, none of whom is widely read by German peasants.

The effect of moods such as anxiety and boredom on the philosopher is, by Heidegger's own account, similar to that of technology. So technology may not be as baneful as he suggests: technology is not uncongenial to philosophy, precisely because it extricates us from our native surroundings. Heidegger is of two minds about rootlessness. One mind hates and fears it, the other cultivates and exploits it. BT records the journey of an everyday person who becomes a philosopher, detached from the everyday world. Quite likely some Jewish *philosophers* made the same journey and are as rootless as Heidegger, but his mistake was to project his own rootlessness onto Jews in general.

Glossary

ableben; Ableben to die or decease as a living organism; demise, biological death.

Anwesenheit presence (e.g. of someone at a place or event). Cf. the Greek *parousia*, 'presence' (from *ousia*, 'being, substance').

Augenblick moment, moment of vision.

auslegen; Auslegung to spread or lay out, to interpret; interpretation.

Befindlichkeit state of mind, how one finds oneself, how one is doing, from *(sich) befinden*, 'to find (oneself)', etc. (as in *Wie befinden sie sich?* (1) 'How do you do?' (2) 'How do you feel?') and *befindlich*, 'to be found' in a place.

besorgen; Besorgen to provide, make provision; concern. It applies to one's dealings with tools and equipment.

bilden; Bild to form, shape, constitute, establish, educate; image, picture.

da; das Da there, here; the There.

damals then (in the past), on that former occasion.

dann then (in the future).

dasein; Dasein to be there (in non-Heideggerian German: to exist); *Dasein*, being-there, human being, being human. Heidegger uses *Dasein* to refer *both* to the (concrete) human being *and* to its (abstract) being human. In BT *Dasein* usually refers to an entity, the

133

human being. In lectures Heidegger often speaks of 'human [*menschliche*] Dasein' and 'the Dasein of man'.

destruieren; Destruktion to destroy; destruction. But Heidegger uses these words in a sense close to 'deconstruct(ion)' and perhaps to Hegel's *aufheben, Aufhebung*, meaning 'kick(ing) upstairs', at once 'cancelling, preserving, and elevating'.

eigentlich; Eigentlichkeit authentic, real; authenticity. This is related to the adjective *eigen*, 'own', 'personal'. To be authentic is to be true to one's 'own self', to be one's own person, to do one's own thing.

Ekstase; ekstatisch ecstasis; ecstatic. Literally 'standing forth'.

entschliessen; entschlossen; Entschlossenheit to resolve; resolute; resoluteness. From *schliessen*, 'to close'; hence literally 'to disclose', etc.

erschliessen; Erschlossenheit to disclose; disclosedness.

existieren, occasionally eksistieren; Existenz; existenzial, existenziell; Existenzial lit. to stand forth, to exist; standing forth, existence; existential (adjective); *existentiell*; existential (noun). The adjectives *existenzial* and *existenziell* differ in the same way as *ontologisch* and *ontisch*, but they apply only to Dasein. Choosing to be a soldier rather than a cobbler is an *existentiell* choice. The capacity to make such choices, and the philosopher's understanding of it, are *existential*.

faktisch; Faktizität factical, facticity; similar to 'factual, factuality' but applied only to Dasein, e.g. the sheer fact that one exists.

Fürsorge solicitude, one's attitude to other humans.

Gegenwart; gegenwärtig; gegenwärtigen the present, lit. waiting towards; (in the) present; to make present.

Gerede idle talk, chatter.

geschehen to happen, historize.

Geschichte; geschichtlich; geschichtlichkeit history; historical; historicality. In Heidegger's usage, these words concern history as happening or events, not the study of events (*Historie*). *Geschichte* also means 'story, narrative', and this influences Heidegger's use of it.

Geschick destiny (of a group or community).

gewesen; Gewesenheit having been (past tense of *sein*); having-beenness, the (living) past.

Gewissen conscience. *Gewissen* is related to *gewiss*, 'certain', but BT, 291 dissociates conscience from certainty.

Historie; historisch history, historiography, historiology; historical, historiographical, historiological.

Horizont horizon. But as Heidegger uses it, it means the realm bounded by a horizon or the vantage point from which we can survey such a realm.

jetzt; das Jetzt now; the now, instant.

man; das Man one, they, etc.; the 'they'.

Neugier curiosity, thirst for novelty.

ontisch; ontologisch; Ontologie ontical; ontological; ontology. Proper ontology deals not with beings (*das Seiende*), but with Being (*das Sein*), either the Being of some specific 'region' of beings or, if it is 'fundamental ontology', Being as such. A claim, enquiry, etc. is ontological if it concerns the *Being* of entities, if, roughly, it is *a priori*. It is ontical if it concerns only beings or entities, if, roughly, it is empirical.

reden; Rede to talk; talk, discourse.

Schicksal fate (of an individual).

sein; das Seiende; das Sein to be; the being, the entity, what is, beings, entities; being, Being. The distinction between *das Seiende* ('beings') and *das Sein* ('Being', usually differentiated by initial capital in translations) is crucial. In xxiv and thereafter Heidegger called it the 'ontological difference' (*ontologische Differenz*).

sorgen; Sorge to worry, take care of, provide for, see to; care, worry, trouble, careful attention.

sterben; das Sterben to die; dying.

stimmen; Stimmung to harmonize, to tune, to put someone into a certain mood; tuning, mood, temper, disposition.

Tod; Sein zum Tode; Freiheit zum Tode death; Being towards death; freedom towards death.

Ursprung, ursprünglich; gleichursprünglich source, origin, lit. leap forth; original, primordial; equiprimordial, equally original.

verfallen; das Verfallen to fall, deteriorate; falling, deterioration.

Vergehen; Vergangen; Vergangenheit to pass (away), elapse, disappear; past, gone by, bygone; the (dead) past.

Vorhabe, Vorsicht, Vorgriff fore-having; fore-sight; fore-conception. This 'fore-structure' (*Vorstruktur*) is involved in all interpretation (BT, 327).

vorhanden available, extant, present-at-hand. In contrast to *zuhanden*, it applies to what is (or is seen as) simply there, neutral, colourless, disengaged from human activities and purposes.

Welt; Umwelt; Lebenswelt, in der Welt, innerweltlich; weltlich; Weltlichkeit world; environment, world around (one, us); life-world; in the world (only of Dasein); within the world (only of things other than Dasein); worldly (of the world); worldhood (of the world). Heidegger distinguishes four senses of *Welt*: (1) the aggregate of all present-at-hand entities; (2) the Being of such entities, or a particular 'region' of them (e.g. numbers etc. are 'the world of the mathematician'); (3) the world in which Dasein lives, either the '"public" we-world, or one's "own" closest (domestic) *Umwelt*'; (4) worldhood, the basic structure of a world. He generally uses *Welt* in sense 3 (BT, 64f.).

werfen; geworfen; Geworfenheit throw; thrown; thrownness.

Zeit; zeitlich, Zeitlichkeit; innerzeitig, zeitigen time; temporal (only of Dasein); temporality (only of Dasein); within time (only of what is other than Dasein); to ripen, mature, temporalize (of temporality).

zuhanden ready-to-hand, handy, available for human use. It applies esp. to *Zeug*, tool(s), equipment, gear.

Zukunft; zukünftig the future (as coming towards); future, futural.

zweideutig; Zweideutigkeit ambiguous, double-dealing; ambiguity, duplicity.

Further reading

A good account of Heidegger's life is R. Safranski's *Martin Heidegger: Between Good and Evil* (Cambridge, MA, 1999). *Basic Writings*, ed. D. F. Krell (London, 2nd edn, 1993) is a useful collection of Heidegger's own works, containing the Introduction to BT, OWA, and nine other essays. Some of Heidegger's lectures, especially xx, xxiv, and xxvi, are easier going than BT itself and make a good introduction to it. Heidegger's earliest writings are translated in *Becoming Heidegger: On the Trail of his Early Occasional Writings, 1910-1927*, eds T. Kisiel and T. Sheehan (Evanston, IL, 2007).

There are several commentaries on BT. *Heidegger on Being Human*, by R. Schmitt (New York, 1969), stresses the similarity between Heidegger and Wittgenstein. Also useful are M. Gelven, *A Commentary on Heidegger's 'Being and Time'* (New York, 1970); S. Mulhall, *Heidegger and Being and Time* (London, 1996); and W. Blattner, *Heidegger's 'Being and Time'* (London, 2006). *The Cambridge Companion to Heidegger's Being and Time*, ed. M. Wrathall (Cambridge, 2013) is a fine collection of essays.

R. Polt, *Heidegger: An Introduction* (London, 1999) covers the whole range of Heidegger's thought in a lucid manner. Two collections covering the later as well as the earlier Heidegger are *The Cambridge Companion to Heidegger*, ed. C. Guignon (Cambridge, 2nd edn, 2006), and *A Companion to Heidegger*, eds H. Dreyfus and M. Wrathall (Oxford, 2005).

Publisher's acknowledgement

We are grateful for permission to include the following copyright material in this book.

Chapter 11: Michael Inwood's original essay first appeared as 'Was Heidegger a Semitic Nomad: Projection and Heidegger's Black Notebooks', *Marginalia Review of Books*, 17 February 2015.

The publisher and author have made every effort to trace and contact all copyright holders before publication. If notified, the publisher will be pleased to rectify any errors or omissions at the earliest opportunity.

We are grateful for permission to include the following copyright material in this book.

Chapter 11: Michael Brown, 'Hospital visit' first appeared as 'My Grandad's a proper Nana', Perspectives on Headteachers' Blogs. No thanks. Unpublished; reprinted by kind permission.

The publisher and author have made every effort to trace and contact all copyright holders before publication. If we, the publishers, will be pleased to put right any errors or omissions at the earliest opportunity.

Index

Index

SOCIAL MEDIA
Very Short Introduction

Join our community
www.oup.com/vsi

- Join us online at the official Very Short Introductions **Facebook** page.
- Access the thoughts and musings of our authors with our online **blog**.
- Sign up for our monthly **e-newsletter** to receive information on all new titles publishing that month.
- Browse the full range of Very Short Introductions online.
- Read **extracts** from the Introductions for free.
- If you are a teacher or lecturer you can order inspection copies quickly and simply via our website.